THE ART OF JOB INTERVIEWS

Answers to the Hardest Questions

Sam Choo

First Published by Hope Publishing 2023.

ISBN No.: 978-981-18-7096-5

Contact: sam@hopepublishing.sg

Table of Contents

Introduction

Job interviews can be a daunting experience for many individuals. The pressure to make a good impression and showcase one's skills and experience can leave even the most qualified candidates feeling nervous and uncertain.

However, with the right preparation and mindset, job interviews can also be an opportunity to showcase one's strengths and stand out from the competition.

This book aims to provide readers with a comprehensive guide to answering some of the toughest job interview questions they may encounter in the hiring process.

Drawing on years of experience in recruitment and human resources, we have compiled a list of the most commonly asked interview questions and provided detailed guidance on how to craft effective and compelling responses.

Whether you are a recent graduate just starting out in your career, or an experienced professional looking to take the next step, this book is designed to help you navigate the job interview process with confidence and ease.

With practical tips and real-world examples, we hope to empower readers to showcase their skills and land their dream job. So let's get started on the journey to mastering the toughest job interview questions!

What is the Interviewer Looking For?

If you know the answer, you will be better prepared.

1. Relevant skills and experience:
Your skills and experience should align with the requirements of the job. They will assess your technical and soft skills to see if you can perform the duties of the position effectively.

Your resume must show that you are proficient enough to perform the role. You have the qualification and the necessary experience to do the job. They do check you have read the job description.

2. Positive attitude and motivation:
They will look for candidates who show enthusiasm and a willingness to learn and grow.

They will ask you to talk about your most interesting project that you mentioned in your resume. They want to see how passionate and knowledgeable you really are. They hope you will feel the same for the company's projects. You ability to articulate how the project worked, would demonstrate whether you are an active and contributing team member, or just reciting a team work.

3. Cultural fit:
They will assess your values, work style, and personality to see if they align with the company's culture.

4. Problem-solving and critical thinking:
They will ask questions that will help them assess a candidate's ability to solve problems and think critically.

They might give you a role play for a given scenario, a problem to solve, take a test or to perform a task. When I applied for a job as a copywriter, they made me write an advertisement in 30 minutes. Luckily I had memorised a 4-step process that enabled me to write a sales page on the spot. A software programmer may be asked to write codes, for example, to sort a list of numbers.

5. Communication and interpersonal skills:
They will look for candidates who are able to articulate their thoughts clearly and work well with others.

They might disagree with you, or criticise you to see your reaction. Are you calm and composed under pressure? Do you accept feedback readily? Are you able to defend your point of view with persuasion?

6. Adaptability and flexibility:
They will ask questions that will help them understand how a candidate handles change and uncertainty.

7. Work ethic and reliability:
They will look for candidates who demonstrate a commitment to their work and a track record of reliability.

By assessing these qualities and traits, they can determine if a candidate is a good fit for the role and the company culture.

How to Prepare for the Job Interview

If I were to ask you if you enjoyed job interviews, a majority of you would answer no. And I can't blame you for it. They are often intimidating and make you very nervous. But you know you have to do it. Question is – are you prepared for your next job interview?

In order to get ready to face what's to come, you should start taking the effort to make yourself stand out from other interviewees. Here are some ways you can do so:

1. Research on the company

Research on the company's background. What do they do? How long have they been around? What's their value, mission and vision? What do they sell? What's their culture like?

Use the company's name through Google, LinkedIn and social media. Connect to current employees and past employees, using polite customized connection request. Send them a message, and ask if they are willing to share about the company work culture. See whether any recent mentioned in the newspapers, whether mainstream or online reporting websites. Create a google alert of the company.

2. Google your name

Your potential employers may conduct their research on you before they hire you. Manage your online reputation by googling your name to make sure you do not have any negative posts or photos.

3. Prepare a list of questions

Study this book and make sure you know how to answer the questions. Some of the typical questions are:

- Tell me about yourself
- Why are you applying for this job
- Why did you leave your last job?
- What's your greatest weakness?
- Why do see yourself five years from now?

Mastering Your First Impression During the Interview

The interviewer takes about ten seconds in the beginning of the interview to size you up and form an impression of you. How you present yourself during this time is super important and can make or break your chances of getting the job. So, it's crucial that you make a good impression in those first few seconds to set yourself up for success.

The unofficial gatekeepers

In some organisations, the unofficial gatekeeper, may decide your fate. Always be polite to the receptionist, security guard and the admin staff. The interviewer may take their impressions very seriously.

Punctuality

Arrive at least 30 minutes earlier. Go to the toilet, freshen up, take mouthwash to gargle, and wipe or wash your face if you have an oily complexion or sweat beads. Do not smoke at least 30 minutes before the interview, as cigarette smoke lingers on your breath and clothing. Don't eat chicken rice with garlic chili before the interview. Eat a breath mint and bring a small bottle of water. Take a writing pad and pens and print out 3 copies of your resume. If you're late, it leaves a bad first impression, and they'll often pass on you. If the location is somewhere you are not familiar with, research well on how to get there. Use Google Maps to get up-to-date directions.

Grooming

Don't forget to tidy up your hands and fingernails. Make sure your hair is well-combed and looking neat. Polish your shoes and wear socks with no holes. Some offices require you to take off your shoes. Don't wear too strong perfume and always shower in the morning. You normally cannot smell your own body odour/bad breath as you are already too used to it.

Attire

Dress formally or appropriately for the interviews. Tone down flashy colors. Ties are almost no longer necessary nowadays (except in banks), but a simple jacket or blazer does wonders to make you stand out from the others. You can always peel off layers, but it's difficult to dress up if you did not bring it.

Handshake

Strike a balance between firmness and not crushing the interviewer's hand. Make sure to engage in a full handshake, not just a finger grip. If you tend to have sweaty palms, it's a good idea to carry a handkerchief to wipe them before entering the interview room.

Body language

Be mindful of your body language and posture. Avoid slouching or sitting in a vulgar manner as it can give off a negative impression. Try to lean forward slightly (but not too much!) and maintain a positive demeanor.

Don't cross your leg and start shaking. Don't cross your hands while sitting. If you are cold, this is when the jacket you have brought along comes in handy. Keep your hands above/on the table. Keeping them hidden under the table may give the impression you have something to hide.

Verbal communication

Avoid speaking too softly, which can raise confidence issues, or too loudly, which can be overwhelming. Instead, try to match the volume of the interviewer's speech.

It's best to refrain from using vulgar language, even mild ones such as "damn," "hell," or synonyms of words like "shit." These words can give the interviewer the wrong impression of your character.

Drinking enough water will prevent your voice from cracking or choking up during the interview. However, be careful not to drink too much and risk needing to use the washroom during the interview.

If they ask if you need water or coffee, always accept water. Interviewers always feel nice that they have done something to make the interviewee feel welcome, and it gives you opportunities to make small talk to get everyone comfortable. Yes, some interviewers may also be nervous, especially if they have not interviewed anyone for some time.

Interaction

Honesty is the best policy. It's important not to lie during an interview. If you don't know the answer to a question, it's perfectly acceptable to admit it. Add by saying, "Let me get back to you on the answer/solution tonight and send it together with your thank-you letter/email."

Attempting to bluff your way through an interview is a sure-fire way to torpedo your chances. Interviewers value authenticity over perfection.

When answering questions, it's best to provide a direct response without unnecessary elaboration unless prompted to do so.

It's also wise to let the interviewer do most of the talking. The more they speak, the less you'll need to. This can help to alleviate any potential nerves.

What NOT to Say or Do During a Job Interview

1. Do not misspell the company's name. If you do not know how to pronounce the company name, it is okay to ask the interviewer how to pronounce it and repeat it a few times until you get it right. It can serve as an icebreaker too.

2. Do not show your ignorance about the role you apply for and the company.

3. Don't ask them what the company does. Ask Google; Google is your best friend.

4. NEVER badmouth your ex-employer or ex-colleagues, actually never badmouth anyone.

5. Do not say you are nervous. Lack of confidence is not a good sign.

6. Do not say, "I'll do whatever". It shows you are desperate enough to do anything.

7. Do not apologise for your lack of experience. Do not draw attention to your weakness.

8. Do not say, "it's on my resume." The interviewers want you to express yourself verbally.

9. Do not say, "Yes! I have an answer for that." Interviewers want a conversation not a memorised script to answer every question.

10. Try not to say, "I don't know." At least try to make a guess. A suggested answer is, "I am not an expert in this area, but based on my experience or knowledge, I would say..."

11. Don't ask what are the perks. It is not the right time.

12. Do not say you have no questions for the interviewer. It shows lack of interest to learn more. Always prepare at least 5 to 10 questions (as sometimes the question may already be answered during the conversation) before the interview and ask at least 3 of them.

13. Don't tell them your ambition to start your own business as soon as possible because they want you to stay longer, and not use them as a stepping stone.

14. No swearing, no 'f' word, no 'what the hell". Interviewer can use them but not you.

15. Don't tell them your sob story about how you are going through a tough time because they don't want your personal life to affect your work. So just talk about professional life, and not your personal problems.

16. Never be late for the appointment.

17. What do you say when you do not Know how to answer the question? Don't lie. Don't ramble. It's OK to admit you haven't yet acquired a specific skill or faced a certain problem. You can say, " I don't know that yet, but I am willing to learn."

Categories of Questions

The interview questions can be grouped into the following categories.

#1: Behavioral questions:

These questions aim to understand how you have behaved in past situations and how you might behave in similar situations in the future. the interviewer might ask you to talk about a specific situation at work where you faced a problem and how you dealt with it. These inquiries often take the form of "Tell me about a time…" Examples include: "Describe a time when you had to deal with a difficult co-worker" and "What has been your biggest challenge and how did you overcome it?"

A recommended way to answer behavioural interview questions is to use the STAR format.

S: SITUATION

Set the scene and give the necessary details of your example.

T: TASK

Explain the challenge or goal you faced. Describe what your responsibility was in that situation

A: ACTION

Explain exactly what steps you took to address it.

R: RESULT

Share what outcomes your actions achieved.

#2: Skills and experience questions:

These questions focus on your past experiences, skills, and knowledge. Examples include: "What is your experience with customer service?" and "What is your experience with data analysis?"

Use the STAR method to answer these questions. Use a variety of experiences, such as work, internships, volunteering, or even personal projects, to showcase your abilities. Tailor your response. Customize your answer to the specific company and role, emphasizing how your skills and experiences are relevant to the job and how they can benefit the employer.

#3: Motivation and career goals questions:

These questions aim to understand your motivation for applying to the role and your long-term career goals. Examples include: "Why are you interested in this role?" and "What are your long-term career goals?"

Showcase your ambition, enthusiasm, and alignment with the company's objectives. Convey your excitement and passion for the opportunity, and express your eagerness to learn and grow within the company. Ensure your career goals are achievable within the context of the company and industry. Unrealistic goals may come across as naive or disingenuous.

Rehearse your answer out loud to ensure you can deliver it confidently, concisely, and naturally.

#4: Interpersonal and communication questions:
These questions focus on your ability to collaborate and communicate effectively with others. "How do you handle conflict with co-workers?" is one example. as well as "What is your leadership style?"

Use the STAR method to organize your answers when talking about how you handle different communication situations, such as working through disagreements, cooperating with others, convincing people, or paying close attention to what someone is saying. Talk about your best qualities and focus on the communication skills that matter most for the job. Show that you can understand and adjust to other people's viewpoints, feelings, and ways of communicating.

Practice delivering your answers out loud to ensure you can express yourself clearly and concisely. Avoid rambling and stay focused on the key points.

#5: Technical and industry-specific questions:
These questions aim to understand your knowledge of specific technical or industry-related topics. Examples include: "What is your experience with social media marketing?" and "What is your experience with blockchain technology?"

Stay informed about the latest developments in your industry, as well as any new tools, techniques, or best practices. Brush up on relevant concepts, tools, technologies, and industry trends.

Provide real-world examples to illustrate your technical knowledge and industry-specific experience. Discuss projects, tasks, or situations where you've applied your skills effectively. For scenario-based technical questions, use the STAR method.

Emphasize your ability to troubleshoot, analyze, and find solutions to technical and industry-specific challenges. Admit when you don't know. If you're unsure of an answer, be honest about it.

In conclusion, by categorizing the questions, you can better understand the interviewer's objectives and prepare more effectively for the interview.

Behavioral Questions:

These questions aim to understand how you have behaved in past situations and how you might behave in similar situations in the future.

Yourself

Question: *Tell me about yourself*

Similar interview questions:
- *Tell me more about who you are*
- *How would other people describe you?*
- *Could you please walk me through your CV?*
- *I have your CV in front of me, but I'd like to hear more about you.*
- *Could you tell me more about your career journey so far?*
- *Tell me a little bit more about your background.*

Why the interviewer is asking this question:
This is the most commonly asked interview question. It is often used as an opening question. This question is often used as an icebreaker to get the conversation flowing, and to give the interviewer a chance to learn a little more about you beyond what's on your resume.

It's not necessarily a question about your personal life or hobbies, but rather an opportunity to share your professional story and career aspirations. One of their aims is to get you talking and to learn more about your personality, work style, and experience. The interviewer can use this information to gain a better understanding of your strengths, weaknesses, and overall fit for the position.

The question is open-ended and allows you to share information about your background, education, work experience, and personal interests.

The interviewer does not want to know all the details about you from birth forward. They are specifically focused on who you are in relation to the specific job for which you are applying. The interviewer is effectively asking: "Tell me about your background on your resume in more detail."

The best approach to answering this question:
In just two minutes, tell the company about your background, achievements, and why you matter to them. The purpose is to prove your reliability and explain why they should be interested in you. Connect with them by relating your experience to their interests and showing how you can help their organization.

To begin, introduce yourself by stating your profession and how you assist individuals or companies in achieving specific goals and outcomes. For example, "I'm a marketing specialist. I help businesses reach their target audience to increase sales and revenue."

Next, establish your credibility by highlighting your previous work and life experience, showcasing your expertise. Discuss the projects you've worked on and the notable individuals you've collaborated with. This demonstrates that you're uniquely qualified to perform the required tasks.

Lastly, explain why they should care about you by highlighting how your work will benefit them. Share a testimonial of how others have benefited from your work, and explain how you can do the same for them.

It's essential to practice your answer, so it rolls off your tongue smoothly when you're caught off guard with this question. Remember, it's all about establishing a connection, showcasing your expertise, and demonstrating how you can be an asset to their organization.

A few other tips to keep in mind:
Keep your answer concise and focused on your professional experience. You don't need to go into too much detail about your personal life or hobbies unless they are directly relevant to the job you're interviewing for.

Be honest and authentic in your response. Don't try to make yourself sound like someone you're not, as this could come across as insincere.

Use it as an opportunity to build rapport with the interviewer.

Talk first about your preparation for the role and then focus in tightly on what makes you the best candidate for the role. Keep your initial answer short, about 2-3 minutes at most.

Try to highlight qualities or experiences that are particularly relevant to the job you're applying for. For example, if the job requires strong communication skills, you might highlight a time when you led a successful project or presentation.

Before your interview, try to rehearse for one to two minutes about who you are, what you've done and why you're interested in the role you're interviewing for.

An example of how to best answer this question:
When answering this question, it's helpful to follow a structure that highlights your relevant experience, skills, and accomplishments. Here's an example:

"I'm [your name], and I've been working in [your industry] for [number of years]. In my current role at [current company], I've gained experience in [relevant skill or responsibility], which has allowed me to [accomplishment or impact]. Prior to that, I worked at [previous company] where I [relevant accomplishment or responsibility]. Overall, I'm passionate about [what motivates you in your work] and I'm excited to explore opportunities that allow me to continue to grow and develop in my career."

Here's another example:
"I worked hard in school and at my job to prepare myself for a successful career as a [profession name]. I got my [degree name] from [university name], and soon after I graduated, I started working at [organization name]. To get better at my job, I passed the [exam name] on my first try and have since advanced in my career. Recently, I got promoted to [current position name], where I get to share what I know with others. I was even chosen to train new employees in our area on our latest project, which was

a great experience for me."
An example of how you should not answer this question:
When getting ready to answer the "Tell me about yourself" interview question, you should avoid these mistakes.
First, don't just repeat what's already written in your resume. Instead, focus on points that are related to the job you're applying for.

Second, avoid sharing personal details like your marital status or whether you have children.

Lastly, don't talk about topics that might be controversial, like your political or religious beliefs.

* * *

Question: *If I were to ask your boss/co-worker to describe you, what would they say?*

Similar interview questions:
* *How would other people describe you?*

Why the interviewer is asking this question:
The interviewer is asking about your qualities and work ethic from the perspective of your boss. They want to know how your boss would describe you and what kind of employee you are. This question allows the interviewer to gain insight into your strengths, weaknesses, and overall performance. The interviewer is looking at your ability to view yourself from an external perspective.

The best approach to answering this question:
Be ready to answer the follow-up question of "Why do you think they would say that?"

Highlight your strengths and qualities that would be relevant to the position you are applying for.

The best approach to answering this question is to be able to back it up with a written letter of recommendation, awards or other performance documentation.

An example of how to best answer this question:
"If you asked my boss/co-worker to describe me, they would probably say that I am a dependable team player who is always willing to go the extra mile to get things done. They might also mention my attention to detail and my ability to prioritize tasks effectively to ensure that projects are completed on time and to a

high standard."

An example of how you should not answer this question:
"You don't need to ask them, I am sure they think I am the best employee they have ever had."

* * *

Question: If you had to live your life over again, what one thing would you change?
Similar interview questions:

- *Do you have any regrets in your life?*
- *Tell me about a part of your life that didn't work out as you had planned.*
- *If you died tomorrow, what would you felt was left unaccomplished in your life?*

Why the interviewer is asking this question:
The interviewer wants to know if you know yourself well enough, identify areas for improvement, whether you can reflect on your life decisions, and how you go about making changes to improve yourself.

The best approach to answering this question:
Choose something that is not too personal or sensitive and to focus on what you have learned from the experience.

Be wise in how you pick out which regret or shortcoming in your life you choose to expose to the interviewer. It should be one that was truly a shortcoming, but has not had a significant impact on your preparation for your career. And do not, under any circumstances, select a personal regret. Keep it professional. Focus on education and experience. Then talk about what you are doing to make up for the shortcoming.

An example of how to best answer this question:
"If I had to live my life over again, I would have focused more on learning new skills and expanding my knowledge in different areas. While I have always been interested in learning and personal growth, I think

there were times in my life when I was too focused on other priorities and missed out on some opportunities to learn new things.

However, I have learned from this experience and have made changes in my life to prioritize learning and personal growth. For example, I have started taking courses in [specific area of interest] and have been attending workshops and conferences to learn from experts in my field.

I believe that continuous learning and personal growth are important for both personal and professional development, and I am committed to making it a priority in my life going forward."

Example:
"If I had to choose one regret in my life, it would be not focusing on my chosen career path earlier. As you can see from my resume, I earned a Bachelor's degree in English. At that time, I wasn't entirely sure what I wanted to pursue as a career.

However, during my final year of college, I had the good fortune of meeting a woman who became an early mentor for me. She provided valuable guidance in selecting a career path and helped me focus my last year of college by taking electives that would better prepare me for a future career in the insurance industry. Thanks to her guidance, I was able to make a successful transition to my current career and I've been grateful for her help ever since."

An example of how you should not answer this question:
"I am content with the way things have happened in my life and would not want to change anything. I believe that everything occurs for a reason."

Challenges

Question: What challenges have you faced in your previous job?

Similar interview questions:
- *Tell me more about who you are*
- *How have you dealt with challenging situations in the past?*
- *What has been your biggest challenge and how did you overcome it?*

Why the interviewer is asking this question:
The interviewer wants to know three things: Can you can solve problems, recover from setbacks, and deal with difficult situations?

The best approach to answering this question:
Give an instance of a particular difficulty you faced at your previous job. Explain the situation and the actions you took to solve the challenge. Emphasize how you conquered the difficulty, what you learned from the experience, and how you utilized that knowledge to enhance your skills or work approach.

An example of how to best answer this question:
As an example, you could describe a situation where you had to meet a challenging deadline for a project, and the project requirements and schedule kept changing. You can explain how you coped with the situation by breaking down the project into smaller tasks, keeping in touch with team members and stakeholders, and being adaptable and flexible in your approach.

An example of how you should not answer this question:
Avoid speaking negatively about previous employers or colleagues when discussing challenges, and instead focus on the positive aspects of the experience and how it helped the candidate grow and develop their skills.

Example:
"My previous job was a walk in the park. No significant challenges, no hurdles to overcome, just smooth sailing all the way. I handled everything like a boss, and the job was practically a piece of cake."

Handling Difficult People

Question: Describe a time when you had to deal with a difficult co-workers.

Similar interview questions:
- *Tell me about a time when you had to handle a difficult situation with a co-worker or supervisor.*
- *Tell me about a time when you had to work with a difficult team member, and how you handled it.*

Why the interviewer is asking this question:
The intention is to test your ability to work collaboratively with others, handle difficult situations, and communicate effectively.

The best approach to answering this question:
Provide an example of a specific situation where you had to deal with a difficult co-worker and explain how you handled it. You should focus on how you resolved the situation in a professional and respectful manner, while also achieving the desired outcome.

An example of how to best answer this question:
For example, you could say that you once had a co-worker who was constantly late to team meetings and not completing their assigned tasks on time. You could explain that you scheduled a one-on-one meeting with the co-worker to discuss the issue and express your concerns in a calm and constructive way. You could also describe how you worked collaboratively with the co-worker to find solutions, such as breaking down tasks into smaller parts,

setting clear deadlines, and checking in regularly to monitor progress.

An example of how you should not answer this question:
Remain professional and avoid speaking negatively about the difficult co-worker when answering this question. The candidate should also emphasize their ability to work collaboratively and communicate effectively, while also highlighting the positive outcomes achieved as a result of their efforts.

Example:
"I haven't really had any difficult co-workers in the past. I get along with everyone, and I don't like to get involved in any office politics or drama."

* * *

Question: How would you deal with a difficult customer?

Why the interviewer is asking this question:
The interviewer wants to know how you handle challenging customers and how you can resolve conflicts in a professional and positive manner.

The best approach to answering this question:
You should describe specific strategies you use to handle difficult customers, such as active listening, empathizing, and finding mutually acceptable solutions. You should also explain how you manage your own emotions and remain calm and composed during challenging situations.

An example of how to best answer this question:
You could say that you would begin by carefully listening to the customer's concerns and empathizing with their point of view. You could explain that you would take a problem-solving approach, asking clarifying questions and working collaboratively with the customer to find a solution that meets their needs and expectations.

An example of how you should not answer this question:
"I would tell them to calm down and stop being difficult. If that doesn't work, I would tell them I don't have time for this and walk away."

Stress Management

Question: How do you handle stress in the workplace?

Why the interviewer is asking this question:
The question aims to understand your ability to manage stress and pressure in the workplace.

The best approach to answering this question:
Describe specific strategies you use to manage stress in a healthy and effective way. Emphasize self-awareness and the ability to recognize when stress levels are becoming overwhelming.

For example, you describe a situation when you had a lot of workloads but you still managed to deliver the work without panicking.

An example of how to best answer this question:
You could say that you practice regular exercise or meditation to manage stress, or you take breaks throughout the day to engage in activities that help you recharge. You could also explain how you prioritize tasks, delegate responsibilities, and set realistic goals to manage workload and avoid feeling overwhelmed.

An example of how you should not answer this question:
Avoid providing answers that suggest that you cannot handle stress, as this could negatively impact your chances of being hired. Instead, emphasize your ability to stay focused and productive during high-pressure situations, while also taking care of your physical and emotional well-being.

Example:
"I don't really get stressed out at work. I'm pretty laid back, and I don't let things bother me too much. If things do get too overwhelming, I just take a break and go for a walk."

Decision Making

Question: Describe a time when you had to make a difficult decision.

Why the interviewer is asking this question:
The interviewer wants to know how good you are at making decisions and handling tough situations. This question helps them see how you solve problems, think critically, and deal with stress and pressure.

The best approach to answering this question:
Provide a specific example of a difficult decision you had to make in the past. Provide the context of the situation, the options you had, and the factors that influenced your decision. Explain how you weighed the pros and cons of each option and ultimately decided on a course of action. Be sure to highlight any positive outcomes that resulted from your decision and any lessons learned from the experience.

An example of how to best answer this question:
"When I was a project manager, I faced a tough decision where I had to choose between delaying the project or moving ahead with a less-than-perfect solution. We had an issue that could have affected the project's success, and it was up to me to make the right decision. I talked to my team and other people involved, weighed the pros and cons of each option, and decided to go with the less-than-perfect solution. It helped us complete the project on time and meet our goals. This experience taught me how vital it is to make hard decisions quickly and seek others' opinions."

An example of how you should not answer this question:

I am having trouble recalling any instance where I had to make a difficult decision. I typically adhere to the employer's guidelines and policies, and I haven't faced any significant challenges that needed me to make a tough choice.

Coping with Failure

Question: Tell me about a time when you failed

Similar interview questions:
- *What has been your greatest failure, and what did you learn from it?*

Why the interviewer is asking this question:
The interviewer is looking to see if you can handle failure, learn from your mistakes, and accept responsibility for your actions. They want to see if you can bounce back from setbacks.

What the interviewer wants to hear is not so much your story of failing, but more about what you learned from it and how you used that knowledge to approach things in a better way.

The best approach to answering this question:
Provide an example of a specific failure you experienced, and explain what went wrong and why. Describe the steps you took to address the failure and the lessons you learned from the experience.

Search for moments when you discover or learn something new, when you realize something needs to change, or when you make progress towards getting better. Emphasis the correction, not the failure.

Avoid blaming others or making excuses for the failure when answering this question. Focus on how you took ownership of the situation and learned from your mistakes to improve your performance in the future.

Use the STAR (Situation, Task, Action, Result) method.

Don't draw attention to a character flaw. Instead, choose a non-critical miscalculation. Maybe the event did not go as planned because of circumstances beyond your control. Maybe you miss the target set by your boss. Maybe your new strategy was not as effective as you expected.

Relate a team failure, not your failure as an individual. A team failure is more excusable. There was a consensus among the members in making the decision even though you did not agree to it.

Pick a low-consequence event with a low stake, not a catastrophic one.

Say it briefly. Skip the unnecessary details.

What you do want to mention are things that are truly beyond any human being's control. For instance, you can talk about how an event you thoroughly planned got cancelled due to stormy weather or how you were unable to fulfil a client's requirement because the requested product was unavailable. It's important to maintain a positive tone of voice so that your interviewers know that although you were disappointed with the outcome, you have moved on and are willing to learn from the experience.

An example of how to best answer this question:
You could say that you once missed a deadline for a project due to poor time management, and that you had to go back to your team members and

stakeholders to apologize and explain the situation. You could explain that you took responsibility for your mistake and worked collaboratively with the team to find solutions, such as re-prioritizing tasks and working overtime to catch up.

Example:
"During my first year of working as a project manager, I was leading a team on a software development project. We had a tight deadline and were working long hours to meet it. Unfortunately, due to poor communication and a lack of clarity around roles and responsibilities, we fell behind schedule, and the project was delivered two weeks late.

After this experience, I realized the importance of clear communication and delegating responsibilities. I took the initiative to schedule regular team meetings, clarified expectations, and developed a project management plan that accounted for potential setbacks. As a result, our team delivered the next project on time and with improved quality."

An example of how you should not answer this question:
"I rarely fail at anything. I always complete my projects on time and with great care."

This answer comes across as arrogant and may make the interviewer doubt your ability to take ownership of mistakes and learn from them.

* * *

Question: How do you handle failure?

Why the interviewer is asking this question:
The interviewer is asking this question to assess the candidate's ability to handle setbacks and adversity in the workplace. This question allows the interviewer to evaluate the candidate's resilience, adaptability, and problem-solving skills. Employers look for candidates who can handle failure constructively and use it as an opportunity to learn and grow.

The best approach to answering this question:
Provide a specific example of a time when you experienced failure in the workplace and how you handled it. Explain how you reacted to the situation, what steps you took to learn from the experience, and what you did to move forward. Be sure to emphasize any positive outcomes that resulted from the experience, such as newfound skills, lessons learned, or a stronger resolve to succeed.

An example of how to best answer this question:
"If I encounter a failure, I try to learn from it and figure out what went wrong. I also look for feedback and advice from others so I can improve. I don't dwell on the failure too much and try to move forward with a positive attitude."

An example of how you should not answer this question:
"I have a difficult time accepting failure. It irritates me, and I frequently dwell on my mistakes. I don't like failing, so I avoid taking risks that could lead to failure."

Feedback

Question: What is the most difficult feedback you have ever received, and how did you respond?

Why the interviewer is asking this question:
The aim of this question is to assess your ability to receive constructive feedback and use it to improve your performance. The interviewer wants to evaluate your openness to criticism, emotional intelligence, and ability to handle difficult conversations at work. Employers seek candidates who can receive feedback gracefully and use it to grow and develop.

The best approach to answering this question:
Can you recall a time when you received critical feedback? If so, describe the feedback you received, how it was delivered, and how you reacted at first. Explain how you processed the feedback, how you dealt with the problem, and what you learned from the experience. It is critical to emphasize any positive outcomes that occurred as a result of the feedback, such as improved skills or a stronger relationship with the person who provided the feedback.

An example of how to best answer this question:
"I received some difficult feedback during my last performance review where my manager pointed out that I tended to micromanage my team, which led to a sense of mistrust and disengagement. Although I was initially defensive and upset, I decided to take the feedback seriously and reflect on it. After speaking with my team and developing a plan to delegate more effectively and provide more autonomy, I saw significant improvements in team morale and

performance. Overall, the experience taught me the importance of listening to feedback and using it to improve myself."

Example:
"Once, my manager gave me feedback that my communication skills needed improvement, which was hard to hear since I thought I was good at it. However, I took it seriously and started improving by taking courses, getting feedback from colleagues, and practicing my skills. I also set specific goals with my manager and received regular feedback on my progress. Although it was tough to hear, I saw it as a valuable learning experience that helped me grow."

An example of how you should not answer this question:
"I can't really think of a time when I received difficult feedback. I usually just do my job and don't pay much attention to what others think."

Deadline

Question: Describe a time when you had to work on a project with a tight deadline, and how you managed to complete it.

Why the interviewer is asking this question:
The interviewer wants to know if you can work under pressure, manage your time well, and meet deadlines. With this question, they will assess your project management, problem-solving, and teamwork abilities.

The best approach to answering this question:
Start by explaining the project you worked on, including what you were supposed to deliver, the deadline, and any other important details.

Highlight the challenge you faced, describing what made the deadline tight and why it was difficult.

Explain how you approached the situation, detailing the steps you took to manage your time, prioritize tasks, and stay organized. You can also discuss any innovative strategies you used to work more efficiently.

Provide examples of specific actions you took to meet the deadline, such as delegating tasks, working longer hours, or simplifying processes.

Finally, discuss the outcome of the project. Did you complete it on time, and was the work of high quality? Share any positive feedback you received from stakeholders.

An example of how to best answer this question:
"In my last job, I was put in charge of planning a big company event that had to be done in just three weeks. It was a lot of work, from finding a good venue and food to inviting guests and making sure people knew about the event.

The hard part was getting everything done in such a short amount of time while still making sure the event was good. To deal with this, I made a plan with specific timelines for when things needed to be done, and I focused on the tasks that were most important or needed to be done first.

I also talked with my team a lot to figure out who should do what, and we had meetings every day to make sure everything was going well.
To make things easier, I made some templates for things like invitations and advertising that we could use again and again.

In the end, we were able to put on a great event that everyone really enjoyed. I learned that it's important to plan things out and work together as a team to get things done."

An example of how you should not answer this question:
"I don't really have an example of a project with a tight deadline. I usually just take my time and make sure everything is done right, even if it takes longer than expected."

Adapting to Change

Question: Give me an example of a time when you had to adapt to a new situation quickly.

Why the interviewer is asking this question:
The interviewer wants to know if you can adjust to new situations promptly and efficiently. They want to evaluate your problem-solving skills, how you handle stress, and if you have a growth mindset. Employers value candidates who can adapt to change with ease and flexibility.

The best approach to answering this question:
Share a specific instance where you displayed flexibility and adaptability in response to unexpected challenges. Begin by describing the situation, including what changed and how it affected the project or task at hand. Detail the steps you took to adapt, including how you evaluated the situation, brainstormed potential solutions, and executed a plan of action. Make sure to emphasize any positive outcomes that resulted from your adaptability, such as improved productivity, strengthened teamwork, or better outcomes.

An example of how to best answer this question:
"I worked as a sales representative, and was suddenly tasked with managing a new territory that had been underperforming for several quarters. To adapt, I researched the territory's history, developed a new sales strategy, and worked closely with the sales team to identify new leads and opportunities. This led to a 30% increase in sales within the first quarter and positive feedback from customers and management."

An example of how you should not answer this question:
"I don't really like to adapt to new situations quickly. I prefer to take my time and make sure everything is done right."

Risk taking

Question: Tell me about a time when you had to take a calculated risk to achieve a goal.

Why the interviewer is asking this question:
The interviewer wants to evaluate if you can make informed decisions while taking risks to achieve your goals. They want to see if you can handle ambiguity and take initiative. Employers prefer candidates who take calculated risks to achieve success, rather than those who are too cautious or impulsive.

The best approach to answering this question:
To showcase your ability to take calculated risks, it's important to provide a specific example from your past work experience. Start by describing the situation and goal, then explain the risk you took and the rationale for taking it. Finally, discuss the outcome of the risk and any lessons learned. This will demonstrate your ability to make strategic decisions that achieve business goals while also managing risk effectively.

An example of how to best answer this question:
As a project manager for a new product launch, I faced a tight deadline and limited budget, so I proposed a calculated risk of outsourcing some of the work to a third-party vendor, worked closely with them, and established clear communication channels to monitor progress. The outcome was successful as we were able to meet our deadline, launch the product successfully, and exceed our sales targets, receiving very positive reviews from our customers."

An example of how you should not answer this question:

"I don't like taking risks. I prefer to stick to what I know and what has worked in the past."

Delivering a Difficult Message

Question: Describe a time when you had to communicate a difficult message to a team member or client.

Why the interviewer is asking this question:
The interviewer wants to know how you handle difficult conversations in a professional and effective manner. They want to evaluate your communication skills, ability to empathize, resolve conflicts, and manage emotions. Employers seek candidates who can communicate difficult messages respectfully, empathetically, and clearly while achieving their goals.

The best approach to answering this question:
To answer this question, you can structure your response in the following way:

Set the scene: Provide context for the situation that required you to communicate a difficult message to a team member or client.

Describe the difficult message: Explain what the message was, why it was challenging to deliver, and how you prepared for it.

Share your approach: Discuss how you communicated the message in a clear, respectful, and empathetic manner. Be sure to highlight any strategies or techniques you used to manage the conversation effectively.

Share the outcome: Describe the outcome of the situation, including how the message was received and any steps you took to follow up and ensure that the issue was resolved.

By using this structure, you can demonstrate your communication skills, empathy, and problem-solving abilities, which are highly valued by employers. Remember to use specific and relevant examples from your past work experiences to illustrate your skills and qualities.

An example of how to best answer this question:
"During my time working as a project manager, I had to communicate a difficult message to a team member who was consistently missing deadlines and causing delays in the project. I knew that I needed to address this issue in a direct but respectful way, so I scheduled a meeting with the team member to discuss their performance. During the meeting, I explained the impact of their delays on the project timeline and team morale, and I listened carefully to their perspective. I also provided clear expectations for future deadlines and offered support to help them meet these goals. As a result of this difficult conversation, the team member was able to improve their performance, and the project was completed successfully."

An example of how you should not answer this question:
"I hate having to communicate difficult messages. It makes me uncomfortable and I avoid it whenever possible."

Ethics

Question: Give me an example of a time when you had to deal with an ethical dilemma.

Why the interviewer is asking this question:
The purpose of this question is to evaluate your ethical decision-making skills and values. The interviewer wants to assess your ability to recognize and resolve ethical dilemmas in the workplace, as well as your commitment to doing what is right. Employers value candidates who can make ethical decisions in complex situations and uphold the company's values and reputation.

The best approach to answering this question:
Demonstrate your ethical decision-making skills and your ability to handle difficult situations.

Here are some tips for crafting your answer:

Choose a relevant example: Choose an example that is relevant to the job you are interviewing for. It should demonstrate your ability to handle ethical issues in a professional setting.

Be specific: Provide specific details about the situation, the people involved, and the ethical dilemma you faced. Explain the options you had and the decision you ultimately made.

Explain your thought process: Walk the interviewer through your thought process as you worked through the ethical dilemma. Explain how you weighed the pros and cons of each option and how you arrived at your decision.

Discuss the outcome: After explaining the decision you made, discuss the outcome of the situation. Did your decision resolve the ethical dilemma? Did it have any other consequences?

Lastly, demonstrate how you have implemented the lessons you learned from the experience in future situations and how it has influenced your ethical decision-making process.

Keep in mind that the interviewer is not expecting a flawless response. Instead, they want to see how you navigate ethical dilemmas and how you integrate your learnings into your professional conduct. Be candid, and reflective, and exhibit your capacity to make sound ethical choices in the workplace.

An example of how to best answer this question:
"While working as a sales representative, I was faced with an ethical dilemma when a customer offered me a bribe to expedite their order. I knew that accepting the bribe would be unethical and against company policy, but I also knew that the customer was a valuable client and their order was important. I immediately consulted with my manager to discuss the situation and seek their guidance. My manager commended me for bringing the issue to their attention and reminded me of our company's commitment to ethical business practices. Together, we developed a solution that involved explaining the order process to the customer, and offering alternatives to expedite the order without

compromising ethical standards. This decision not only maintained our company's integrity, but also strengthened our relationship with the customer."

An example of how you should not answer this question:
"I've never faced an ethical dilemma in the workplace. I always know what the right thing to do is."

Skills and Experience Questions:

These questions focus on your past experiences, skills, and knowledge.

Skill

Question: What skills do you have that are relevant to this position?

Similar interview questions:
- *What are your technical skills?*
- *What skills do you bring to the table that are not listed in your resume?*

Why the interviewer is asking this question:
The interviewer wants to know if you meet the qualifications for the job. They want to know if you understand the job requirements and can explain how your skills and experiences align with them. Candidates who can articulate their strengths and demonstrate how their abilities will benefit the company are preferred by employers.

The best approach to answering this question:
This question is asking you to explain how your skills and experiences match the requirements of the job. To answer it well, you should mention the specific skills the job needs, give examples of how you have used those skills in the past, and mention any achievements that show your abilities in those areas.

An example of how to best answer this question:
"My skills and experiences appear to be a good match

for the requirements of this position. For example, I have project management and coordination experience, which I believe will be beneficial in this role. I'm also skilled at communicating with customers and stakeholders to ensure that everyone's needs are met. My previous job required me to problem-solve and communicate effectively on a daily basis. I'm also familiar with relevant software and tools, such as [insert specific software or tools], which I believe will help me perform well in this job."

An example of how you should not answer this question:
"I'm a hard worker and a quick learner, so I'm sure I can pick up any skills necessary for this position."

Experience

Question: What is your experience in this field?

Why the interviewer is asking this question:
The interviewer wants to know if you have the experience and qualifications required for the job. They'll ask about your skills and experience in the field to evaluate your knowledge of the industry and your specific abilities related to the position. Employers want to find candidates who have the right expertise and experience to get the job done well.

The best approach to answering this question:
Give a brief summary of your relevant experience and skills that relate to the job. If you have any certifications or training relevant to the position, mention them too. Talk about any significant projects you have led or been a part of and provide examples of how your skills and experience helped to achieve positive results. Keep your response concise and specific to demonstrate your suitability for the job.

An example of how to best answer this question:
"I have been working in the [industry/field] for [number of years] years, and have developed a deep understanding of the key trends and challenges in the industry. In my previous role at [company], I was responsible for [specific responsibilities related to the job]. I led several successful projects that involved [specific skills related to the job], and was recognized for my contributions to [specific accomplishment related to the job]. Additionally, I have completed [relevant training or certifications], which have equipped me with the necessary skills to perform this

job effectively."

An example of how you should not answer this question:
question:
"I don't have much experience in this field, but I'm a quick learner and I'm sure I can pick up the necessary skills."

Your Competitive Edge

Question: Why should I hire you?

Similar interview questions:
- *What makes you stand out from other candidates?*
- *What sets you apart from other candidates?*
- *What makes you the best candidate for this position?*
- *Why are you the best person for this job?*
- *Why do you deserve this job?*
- *What can you bring to the company?*
- *What can you contribute to this company?*
- *Why should we hire you?*

Why the interviewer is asking this question:
The interviewer will commonly ask this question during job interviews. They want to understand if your skills, qualities, and qualifications align with the requirements of the job and the company's culture. It's an opportunity for you to showcase yourself and make a case for why you're the best fit for the job.

The best approach to answering this question:
Don't be too modest in selling yourself. Quote what others said about you.

Convince the interviewer that you are the best person for this job since you possess all the skills and knowledge that are required for this job role.

Since you don't know who the other candidates are, you cannot compare with them. Highlight your capabilities and achievements that are valuable to the company.

Focus on your education, work experience, skills, aptitudes and abilities which differentiate you from your competition.

Any statements you might make need to be backed up with examples that show how you try are the best person for the position. Your answer should be geared toward meeting the employer's needs, not your personal needs.

Use specific examples. An excellent way to do this is with the STAR method.

An example of how to best answer this question:
"I was awarded the Employee of the Month award as an intern this past summer and was the first intern ever to receive that award. I was given that award over all other nominations of their full-time staff. That award was given due to my delivery on a project that no one else had been able to successfully complete. I not only delivered the project, but I did it while also working on two other projects, both of which were completed during my job one summer as an intern. Let me tell you about the project where I won the award..."

You can say you have extensive experience in [specific skill] have a proven track record of delivering successful projects on time and within budget.

For a leadership position, you can explain that you have excellent communication and leadership skills, and have been recognized for your ability to motivate and inspire team members.

An example of how you should not answer this question:
"Well, I need a job and I think I can do it. Plus, I really need the money."

* * *

Question: Why should I NOT hire you?

Why the interviewer is asking this question:
The interviewer is asking this question to assess the candidate's level of self-awareness and honesty. The question allows the interviewer to evaluate how well the candidate knows their limitations, weaknesses, and areas for improvement. Employers look for candidates who are able to identify their own weaknesses and take steps to address them, rather than trying to hide or deny them.

The best approach to answering this question:
The best approach to answering this question is to provide a honest and self-reflective response. Start by acknowledging any areas in which you may be lacking or any weaknesses you have identified. Be sure to provide specific examples of how you have addressed or are working to improve these areas, such as taking courses, seeking mentorship, or practicing skills outside of work. Highlight any strengths or skills that make up for these weaknesses, and provide examples of how you have successfully applied these strengths in your previous roles or experiences.

An example of how to best answer this question:
"I think one area in which I may struggle is [specific weakness or limitation]. For example, in my previous role at [company], I found it challenging to [specific situation or task]. However, I have been working to improve in this area by [specific steps taken to address the weakness, such as taking courses, seeking mentorship, or practicing skills outside of work]. Additionally, I believe my strengths in [specific skills or qualities] help to make up for this weakness. For

example, in my previous role, I was able to [specific accomplishment or success] by leveraging these strengths."

The answer will be the value that you stand for, and your boundaries are not aligned with the company. So what do you stand for?

Here are my answers.

1. I am not a 'yes' person
If you are looking for people who agree to everything you say, I am not the person for you. If I disagree with you, whether you are the Chairman or President, I will voice my opinion.

2. Working Overtime
I believe in measuring a person's performance by the output, not by the number of hours in the office. I don't believe that an employee has to leave the office only after the boss do so. I don't believe that workers should be working late all the time, unless there are urgent tasks. When an employee works overtime all the time, it means he is not efficient in getting work done or the company is overloading the worker with too much work.

3. Micro management
I don't believe that a supervisor should micro-manage the staff. Staff should be given some leeway. Staff should be trusted as long as they delivers their work properly.

4. Annual assessment

I think that managers should provide feedback as soon as they notice something is wrong instead of waiting for an annual assessment. Waiting until then to give feedback is not effective because employees won't have the chance to improve themselves immediately. It's important to receive feedback in a timely manner so that employees can work on their weaknesses and strive for promotions.

5. Use of vulgar language

I am not a Gary V fan. I don't like people including my superior to use vulgar language when they talk to me.

An example of how you should not answer this question:

"I don't think there's any reason not to hire me. I'm pretty much perfect for the job."

Workload

Question: How do you handle a heavy workload?

Why the interviewer is asking this question:
The interviewer is looking to see if you can handle a heavy workload and work efficiently under pressure. They may inquire about your ability to prioritize tasks and manage your time effectively. This is especially important if your job requires you to work on multiple projects at the same time or meet strict deadlines.

The best approach to answering this question:
The best approach to answering this question is to provide specific examples of how you have managed a heavy workload in the past. Start by outlining your approach to managing a heavy workload, such as breaking tasks into smaller manageable chunks, prioritizing tasks, or creating a schedule. Then, provide examples of how you have applied these strategies in previous roles, highlighting specific accomplishments and successes. Emphasize your ability to remain calm and focused under pressure and your willingness to seek help or delegate tasks when necessary.

An example of how to best answer this question:
"I'm used to handling a heavy workload and have developed strategies to manage it effectively. For example, I break tasks into smaller manageable chunks and prioritize them based on their level of importance and deadline. In my previous role at [company], I was responsible for managing multiple projects simultaneously, and I found it helpful to create a schedule to stay on track. I also made sure to

communicate regularly with my team members and supervisor to ensure that everyone was aware of the workload and deadlines. As a result, I was able to successfully complete all projects on time and within budget."

An example of how you should not answer this question:
"I don't really handle stress well, and a heavy workload tends to overwhelm me."

Time Management

Question: How do you manage your time?

Why the interviewer is asking this question:
The interviewer is asking this question to assess the candidate's ability to manage their time effectively and efficiently. The interviewer wants to know if the candidate can prioritize tasks, meet deadlines, and work efficiently. This question is particularly important for roles that require the candidate to work on multiple projects simultaneously, meet tight deadlines, or work in a fast-paced environment.

The best approach to answering this question:
Provide specific examples of how you have managed your time in the past. Start by outlining your approach to managing your time, such as creating a to-do list, breaking tasks into smaller manageable chunks, or using time-management software. Then, provide examples of how you have applied these strategies in previous roles, highlighting specific accomplishments and successes. Additionally, emphasize your ability to remain focused and meet deadlines, as well as your willingness to adjust your approach to time management based on the needs of the job.

An example of how to best answer this question:
"I'm used to managing my time effectively and have developed strategies to stay organized and productive. For example, I create a to-do list each day and prioritize tasks based on their level of importance and deadline. I also break larger tasks into smaller manageable chunks and schedule regular breaks to

maintain focus. In my previous role at [company], I was responsible for managing multiple projects simultaneously, and I found it helpful to use time-management software to stay on track. As a result, I was able to successfully complete all projects on time and within budget."

An example of how you should not answer this question:
"I don't really have a method for managing my time. I just sort of take things as they come."

Strength

Question: What are your strengths?

Similar interview questions:
- *What is your greatest strength?*
- *What do you do best?*
- *What is an area where you are considered to be an expert?*
- *Is there an area where you are the go-to person on your team?*
- *What is your greatest attribute?*
- "Can you give me an example of how you've used that strength in your job?"

Why the interviewer is asking this question:
The interviewer is curious about your skills and how they can be applied to the job. They want to know what your strengths are and how they can benefit the company. This question assists the interviewer in determining whether you have the necessary skills and abilities for the position.

The best approach to answering this question:
Choose a strength that is relevant to the job you are applying for and provide specific examples of how you have demonstrated that strength in the past. Highlight how this strength can benefit the company and make you a valuable addition to the team.

Here are some examples of strengths:
- Dedicated
- Adaptable
- Creative
- Resourceful

- Problem-Solving
- Ability to work under pressure
- Time management
- Team player
- Leadership
- Communication
- Fast learner
- Analytical skills
- Focus
- Self-starter
- Disciplined
- Reliable
- Patient
- Ambitious
- Efficient
- Growth mindset
- Specialist knowledge/skills
- Hard-working
- Empathetic
- Innovative
- Attention to detail
- Data-driven
- People skills
- Honesty
- Persistent
- Positivity
-

An example of how to best answer this question:
"My greatest strength is my ability to [specific skill or quality], which I believe is crucial for success in this position. For example, in my previous job at [previous company], I was able to [specific achievement or responsibility that demonstrates this skill]. I was able

to achieve this through [specific actions you took to demonstrate this strength].

I believe that this strength can benefit the company by [specific benefits, such as improving productivity or enhancing customer satisfaction]. I am constantly looking for opportunities to develop this strength and to learn new skills that can benefit the company.

Overall, I am confident that my greatest strength can be a valuable asset to the company and that it can help me make a positive contribution to the team."

In this example, the candidate provides a specific strength that is relevant to the job they are applying for. They give an example of how they demonstrated this strength in a previous job and highlight how it can benefit the company. Additionally, they show that they are proactive in developing their skills and learning new things to benefit the company.

Example:
"I think I am a strong leader. I enjoy working with teams and I have good communication skills. When I was a Team Lead at xyz company, my team was the number one sales team in the company for three months running. In fact, later that year I was given a leadership award by management to acknowledge this achievement."

Example:
"I would say that one of my biggest strengths is my empathetic personality. Having worked in Technical Support for over three years, I have helped many different people. During that time, I dealt with many

angry customers. However, even when a customer is being rude and hostile I do my best to help them by being patient, communicating calmly and by practicing active listening. Once the customer feels that someone hears and understands their frustrations, I find that they usually calm down and we can work together to solve their issue."

An example of how you should not answer this question:
Don't say you can solve the Rubik's cube in 10 seconds. It may be a record but it is not relevant to the company's growth.

Weakness

Question: What is your biggest weakness?

Similar interview questions:
- *What are your weaknesses?*
- *In what areas are you the weakest?*
- *What are the areas where you need to improve your skills the most?*
- *Are there areas where you need to develop your skills further?*
- *What would your boss say is the area where you need further improvement?*

Why the interviewer is asking this question:
The interviewer wants to understand your level of self-awareness about areas for improvement, your honesty, and your willingness to learn and grow.

The best approach to answering this question:
Choose a weakness that is not a critical requirement for the job, to show that you are aware of the weakness, and to explain how you are working to overcome it.

Select a weakness that won't make you look incompetent or unable to perform the role. Frame your weakness as a learning moment. Don't reveal too much. Your answer should be brief and to the point.

Be truthful. That doesn't mean you need to present your greatest life weakness or something personal about you. Keep the interview focused on your education and experience. Choose a true weakness, yet choose one which you are actively working to change and improve.

Some coaches suggest presenting a strength as a weakness. This means picking a non-fatal weakness that is actually a strength in disguise. For example: 'I sometimes work so hard that I lose track of time and forget to take breaks like lunch.' Or, 'I'm very focused on my work and sometimes get so absorbed that I don't notice when others have left the office.' This is an old and over-used trick and hiring managers will see right through it.

Qualify your weakness by saying that you are working on rectifying your weakness. It shows your honesty and your effort to improve yourself. Talk about specific steps you have taken or plan to take to overcome this weakness.

While discussing your weakness, try to stay positive and emphasize how you are using this weakness as an opportunity for growth.

Here are some questions that may help you identify your weaknesses:
- Have you ever had difficulty completing a work task? If so, what steps did you take to improve?
- Has a previous supervisor ever given you constructive feedback on areas for improvement?
- Have you worked on a project that required improvement? If yes, what actions did you take to address the issue?
- Are there any particular tasks that you tend to avoid or struggle with?

Here are some examples of weaknesses:
- Lack of Tactfulness
- Trouble Managing Work-Life Balance
- Talkative
- Micromanager
- Harsh Self-Criticism
- Impatience
- Lack of Organization
- Trouble with Delegation
- Timidity
- Indecisiveness
- Fear of Public Speaking
- Poor multitasker
- Teamwork
- Inability to say no
- Playing it safe
- Time management
- Creativity
- Task Delegation
- Focus
- Taking risks
- Lack of confidence
- Trouble asking for help
- Overly sensitive
- Expecting too much from colleagues
- Being too detail-oriented
- Too extraverted
- Too introverted
- Perfectionist
- Procrastination
- Overthinking

An example of how to best answer this question
"My greatest weakness is my tendency to [specific weakness], which I believe can sometimes hinder my ability to [specific task or responsibility]. I am aware of this weakness, and I have been working on improving it by [specific actions you have taken to overcome this weakness].

For example, I have been [specific ways you are addressing the weakness, such as taking a course, seeking feedback, or practicing a skill]. I am also open to feedback and constructive criticism from my colleagues and superiors, which has helped me identify areas for improvement.

Overall, I believe that acknowledging and working on our weaknesses is an important part of personal and professional growth, and I am committed to continuously improving myself in this area."

In this example, the candidate provides a specific weakness that is not critical for the job they are applying for. They show that they are aware of the weakness and are taking steps to address it. Additionally, they highlight their openness to feedback and their commitment to personal and professional growth. This approach shows the interviewer that you are self-aware, willing to learn and grow, and able to recognize areas for improvement.

Explain your weaknesses in a positive light. Some examples include:
- "I am a workaholic. I tend to get so engrossed in work that I forget my meals. I am learning to

balance these two well so I can keep up with my responsibilities and not let health issues come in the way."

- "I feel like I could use more exposure in the customer service line. I have made achievements in the accounts department but I would like to be able to step out and speak to clients more often to build better working relationships overall."

- "I am well-versed in document software but am still learning when it comes to database management systems. I am planning to enrol myself in a class to hone on this skill during my spare time."

An example of how you should NOT answer this question:
Try not to say these:
"I don't know."
"I don't have a weakness."

A reasonable answer could be:
"I don't have a certificate in ____ but I do have the practical experience"
"I am impatient when people do not deliver their work on time or are late for appointment."

Salary Expectation

Question: What are your salary expectations?

Similar interview questions:
- *What kind of salary are you seeking?*
- *What is your current salary?*
- *How much do you need to earn to justify making a move?*
- *Do you have a number in mind for what you want to be earning?*

Why the interviewer is asking this question:
It's important for them to make sure that what they can offer matches your expectations. So, if you ask for too much, it might not work out. Don't worry though, if they bring up the topic of salary, it's usually a good sign that they're interested in hiring you.

The best approach to answering this question:
Do research on the average salary range for the job and industry, and also consider factors such as experience and education. It is important to provide a salary range rather than a specific number, as this shows flexibility and openness to negotiation. The candidate should also emphasize that they are more interested in the overall opportunity and the company culture, and that salary is only one aspect of the job.

Some job seekers give a number when asked about their salary expectations, but this can be risky. If the number is too low, they may not get the salary they could have. But if the number is too high, they may not get the job at all.

Usually, it is best not to be the first one to mention a specific salary amount during a job interview. Instead of giving a number, you can ask the interviewer a question about the salary range for the role.

An example of how to best answer this question:
"I would like to earn as much as possible, but I am willing to negotiate a reasonable salary for the role. Could you please tell me more about the salary range for this position?"

Example:
"I appreciate you asking about my salary expectations. Would you mind sharing the salary range for this position, based on my experience and the role's requirements?"

Example:
"Well, I've done some research on the average salary range for this position in the industry and based on my experience and skills, I am looking for a salary range of $60,000 to $70,000 per year. However, I am open to discussing this further based on the overall opportunity and benefits package. My main focus is finding the right opportunity to grow my career and contribute to a great company culture."

Example:
"I looked into what other people with my experience and skills usually get paid in this job, and I found that it's usually between $X to $Y. However, I'm also interested in learning about the benefits your company offers. Although the exact amount of money is important, what's more important to me is finding

the right job. So I'm open to discussing the details with you."

An example of how you should not answer this question:
"I anticipate earning at least $80,000 per year. That's what I was making at my previous job, and I don't want to go backwards. My top priority is money."

"I want to earn the highest salary possible, like $100K. Can you offer that?"

Hobbies and Interest

Question What are your hobbies and interests?

Why the interviewer is asking this question:
The interviewer is asking about your hobbies and interests to get a better understanding of you as a person and to see if you would be a good fit for the company culture and job requirements. They may also be looking to see if your hobbies and interests could be valuable in the position or if they showcase transferable skills that could benefit the job.

The best approach to answering this question:
To answer this question, be honest and authentic. It's an opportunity to showcase your personality, character, and interests. Remember to maintain a balance between personal interests and professional development. Share hobbies and interests that reflect positive qualities such as discipline, leadership, teamwork, or creativity. It's good to link your hobbies and interests to the skills and qualities required for the position or to the company culture. Avoid mentioning controversial hobbies or interests that could impact your image.

An example of how to best answer this question:
"Some of my hobbies and interests include basketball, hiking, and photography. Basketball has taught me discipline, teamwork, and leadership skills since I was a child. Hiking allows me to connect with nature while also physically challenging myself, which I believe is important for personal growth. I also like photography because it allows me to be creative and express myself visually. These hobbies, I believe, have taught me

valuable skills that I can apply in the workplace, such as teamwork, problem-solving, and creativity."

An example of how you should not answer this question:
"I don't really have any hobbies or interests."

* * *

Question: What are your favorite books or movies?

Why the interviewer is asking this question:
The interviewer wants to know more about your personal interests, hobbies, and cultural background. This question can give them insight into your personality, character, and values. They may also use your response to see if your interests match the company culture or requirements of the job.

The best approach to answering this question:
Provide a genuine and honest response that demonstrates your personality, character, and interests. Try to strike a balance between personal interests and professional development. You should focus on books or movies that have inspired you or have taught you something valuable. Try to relate your favorite books or movies to the skills and qualities required for the position or to the company culture. Avoid mentioning books or movies that may be controversial or could reflect poorly on you.

An example of how to best answer this question:
So, when it comes to books, 'The Alchemist' by Paulo Coelho is my favorite. It's all about following your dreams and discovering your true calling in life, which I find extremely inspiring. It taught me to never give up and to keep going even when things get tough.

In terms of movies, 'The Shawshank Redemption' is unquestionably one of my favorites. It's a timeless story about hope and redemption, which I believe is extremely important. It teaches us that even in the face of adversity, we should never give up and must persevere.

An example of how you should **not** answer this
question:
"I don't really have any favorite books or movies."

Achievement

Question   What   is   your   greatest
achievement/accomplishment?

Similar interview questions:
- *What is your proudest accomplishment?*
- *What is the biggest achievement in your life?*
- *What is the single most important result in your life?*
- *At your future retirement party, what will you look back on as being the most important project or deliverable of your career to date?*
- *What are you most proud of in your career?*
- *What accomplishments have given you the most satisfaction in your life?*
- *At the end of the day, what gives you the most satisfaction in your work?*

Why the interviewer is asking this question:
The question aims to understand the your proudest accomplishment and how you measure success. They want to know your capabilities. They want to see if your achievements are relevant to the position you are applying for and if they can be applied to the company.

Do not, under any circumstances, use a personal accomplishment as your response. Even though you may consider your marriage or your spiritual conversion or the birth of a child or something else in your personal life to be your greatest accomplishment in life, that's not what the interviewer is seeking. This is a career question, not a life question.

The best approach to answering this question:
Choose an achievement that is relevant to the job you are applying for and that demonstrates skills that are important for the position.

Use the S-T-A-R components to answer this question:
S: Situation
T: Task
A: Action you took
R: Results achieved.

It is acceptable to talk about a shared deliverable which was achieved by a team, but be careful to select one where you were a key member for delivery, not simply successful by being part of the team that delivered. You will need to talk specifically about your role in delivery.

One effective way to showcase your accomplishments is by using quantifiable figures. For instance, if you're a salesperson, you could emphasize your success by stating, "I exceeded the sales target of $100,000 in my first three months in the role."

An example of how to best answer this question:
"One of my greatest achievements was [specific achievement], which I completed while working at [previous company]. The project was to [describe project goal], and it was a challenging project that required me to [describe skills used]. I led a team of [number of people] and we worked together to [describe project process and challenges].
In the end, we were able to [describe successful project outcome and impact], which led to [specific business outcomes, such as increased revenue or customer

satisfaction]. I was proud of the work my team and I accomplished, and I received positive feedback from my manager and colleagues.

I believe that this achievement demonstrates my ability to [specific skill or quality], which I think is important for this position. I am confident that I can use this experience and skillset to contribute to the success of your company."

In this example, the candidate chose a specific achievement that demonstrates relevant skills for the position they are applying for. They gave details about the project and the impact it had on the business. In addition, they highlighted how this achievement demonstrates their ability to contribute to the company's success.

Example:

You can say that your greatest achievement was completing a challenging project on time and within budget, which helped the company save money and increase efficiency. You can explain that you used your problem-solving, project management, and communication skills to achieve this goal, and that it aligned with your long-term career goal of becoming a successful project manager.

Example:

You can say that you are most proud of successfully leading a team through a complex project, where they had to overcome numerous challenges and obstacles. This accomplishment could showcase the your leadership skills, problem-solving abilities, and ability to work collaboratively with others, all of which align with your long-term career goals.

An example of how you should not answer this question:
"My greatest accomplishment is that I am still alive after surviving a skydiving accident a few years ago. It was a life-changing experience, and I learned to live life to the fullest and never take anything for granted."

Talking about unrelated accomplishments may not be the best approach as it does not provide insight into how the candidate can add value to the position. It is important to choose a relevant accomplishment that highlights your strengths and capabilities in relation to the job requirements.

Smart

Question: Are you smart?

Similar interview questions:
- *Tell me the best thing about yourself*

Why the interviewer is asking this question:
Asking a question like "Are you smart?" in a job interview is not acceptable or standard practice. It can be viewed as discriminatory and has no relevance to the job requirements. Interviewers should only ask questions related to the job position to evaluate the candidate's skills, experience, and suitability for the role.

The best approach to answering this question:
Reframe the question and focus on your skills, qualifications, and experiences. Avoid directly answering the question as it may come across as arrogant or lacking self-awareness. Instead, you can highlight specific skills and experiences that demonstrate your intelligence and problem-solving abilities.

An example of how to best answer this question:
I am confident that I am qualified for this position. In school and previous jobs, I learned a lot, which helped me develop skills like problem-solving and data analysis. I'm always eager to learn more, and I'm confident that I can make a significant contribution to this organization.

These are the possible answers. Let's examine the response closer.

Response #1: "I am smarter than others."
"I am smarter than my colleagues. They always screw up and I have to save them, such as..."
Mistake: Don't blame people. Egomaniac people will brag.

Response #2: "I am not smart." "I don't really think that I am that smart."
Mistake: Sign of low self-esteem.

Response #3: "My certificates and my past employments prove that I am smart."
It is an objective but cold answer.

Response #4: Walk out of the room.
What an insulting/dumb question!

Response #5: Ask a question.
"What kind of smart is your company looking for?"
"What kind of smarts are you looking for in candidates for this job?"
"What kind of smart do you mean? There are different kinds of intelligence."
'Smart' is a vague term. Smart in what?
"What's the turnover rate in your company?"

Response #6: Use Humour
Call your spouse or friend over the phone if he or she thinks you are smart.
Hang up. and tell the interviewer yes, I am smart.

Response #7: Sarcastic.
"That's not for me to say."
What might be a smart answer?
Let me give a try.

"I am smart enough to know that I don't know everything. That's why I am a lifelong learner."
"I am smart enough to know that everyone know something more than me.
I am smart enough to tap on their expertise by asking them for help."
"I am smart because I learn quickly. And I work hard."
"I am smart enough to be here."

An example of how you should not answer this question:
"Yes, I am very smart. I have an IQ of 140 and have always excelled in academics and every job I have had."

This type of response is not recommended as it comes across as arrogant and lacks humility. Moreover, it does not provide any specific examples of skills or experiences that demonstrate the candidate's intelligence or qualifications for the job.

Motivation and Career Goals Questions:

These questions aim to understand your motivation for applying to the role and your long-term career goals.

Motivation
Question: *What motivates you?*

Similar interview questions:
- *What motivates you to do your best work?*
- *What makes you tick?*
- *What encourages you to do your best work?*
- *What inspires you?*
- *What influences you to be your best?*

Why the interviewer is asking this question:
The interviewer wants to know what drives you to do your best and reach your goals. They want to see if you really care about your work and are willing to put in your best effort. They want to make sure you share the same goals and values as the company and that you are a good fit for the job and the company.

The best approach to answering this question:
Be honest and specific. Avoid general or vague answers such as "money" or "success."

Share what is most gratifying and satisfying about your work. Which aspects in your previous jobs excited and energized you most?

Make sure your motivation is relevant and aligned with your role in the new company. Stay relevant. Pick the ones that are relevant to the role you applied for. For a small startup, you can say that you are motivated to learn new things.

For your preparation, write a list of work in the job description and pick the aspects that excite you.

Stand out with a story. The interviewers must have heard many standard cookies answers. Stand out from the rest with your own stories. Share a brief story about the project that make you feel excited about doing your job.

Give examples: Share specific instances when you were highly motivated and what factors contributed to your success. This could be a project you were particularly proud of or a challenge you overcame. Providing examples helps to illustrate your point and demonstrate your abilities.

Instead of discussing money, it's best to emphasize the importance of doing engaging and fulfilling work, receiving recognition for accomplishments, having the necessary tools and resources to perform tasks effectively, and the potential for future growth and development. Most professionals find doing interesting work as their primary motivator. If the interviewer asks about compensation, acknowledge the importance of salary but reiterate that job satisfaction and engaging work are your primary motivators.

Focus on intrinsic motivation: Talk about what motivates you internally, such as your passion for the work, your desire to learn and grow, or your commitment to excellence. Employers are looking for candidates who are self-driven and have a strong work ethic.

Show alignment with company values: Research the company and its values, and talk about how your own motivations align with those values. This shows that you have a genuine interest in the company and its mission.

An example of how to best answer this question
"I feel motivated when I can help others and make a positive impact. In my last job, I enjoyed resolving customer issues and ensuring they were happy with the service they received. It motivated me to go above and beyond to provide excellent service and exceed their expectations. I believe this same motivation would help me excel in this role and make a difference in the lives of others. I'm also motivated by learning and growing professionally. Setting goals and working towards achieving them keeps me motivated and engaged."

An example of how you should not answer this question:
"I'm solely motivated by money. I always measure my success by the amount of money I earn. If I'm doing well financially, that means I'm doing well overall. If you want me to put in extra effort, offer me more money. That's the only thing that truly motivates me."

Interest

Question: Why are you interested in working for this company?

Similar interview questions:
- *Why do you want to work for our company?*
- *What interests you about this position?*
- Why are you interested in this role?
- *Why do you want to work here?*

Why the interviewer is asking this question:
The intention is to gauge your level of interest and enthusiasm for the company and its mission. They want to see if you have done your research and have a genuine interest in the position and the company culture.

The best approach to answering this question:
There are three fundamental approaches to consider when answering this question:
1. Convey your personal enthusiasm for the company's product, service, or mission.
2. Elaborate on why you find the role's responsibilities appealing and would enjoy performing them.
3. Illustrate how your skills and experience align with the requirements of the position and how you see yourself excelling in the role.

These are the possible reasons for your interest:
- Reputation of the company and leaders
- Their products and services
- The company culture, mission, values and philosophy

- The company's growth and successes
- Specific company initiatives that you admire
- Role at this company that align with your long-term career goals

An example of how to best answer this question:

Here are some ways to express your personal passion for the employer's product, service, or mission:
- "Throughout my career, I have always been drawn to companies that share my values and beliefs. That's why I am excited about the opportunity to work for [company name], which is known for its commitment to [specific cause or mission]."
- "I have been a fan of [company name] for a long time, ever since I first learned about their innovative approach to [product/service]. Their dedication to [specific aspect of the product/service] is truly inspiring, and I would be honored to contribute my skills and expertise to such a forward-thinking organization."
- "I'm really passionate about [specific industry or issue], and that's why I'm excited about the opportunity to work for [company name]. They're known for being a leader in this field and I admire their commitment to [specific aspect of the industry/issue]. I think I could bring a lot of value to their team and contribute to their mission."

Here are some examples of how to show that you enjoy the responsibilities of the role:
- "I think one of my strong suits is teaching and guiding others. I get a lot of satisfaction from

watching people learn and improve, so I'm excited about the chance to work in Learning and Development. It's motivating to think that I could help my colleagues develop their skills and reach their potential, all while contributing to the success of the company."

- "As someone who has always loved writing and editing, I am thrilled to see that these skills are a major part of this job. Whether it's crafting compelling copy for a marketing campaign or polishing up technical documentation, I know that I would enjoy the creative challenge and the chance to make a tangible impact on the company's content."
- "I enjoy analyzing data and using it to make critical decisions. I became interested in this field while working as a research assistant in college and then as a business analyst. It fascinates me how we can learn useful information by analyzing data. In this position, I am looking forward to applying my analytical skills to problems such as creating graphs and making data-driven predictions."

Examples of how your skills and experience can help you succeed in the role:

- "Given my background in X, I am confident that I can quickly learn and apply the necessary skills to excel in this position."
- "I have a proven track record of successfully managing projects and meeting deadlines, which I believe will be valuable in this role."
- "My experience in Y has equipped me with the skills needed to effectively communicate with clients and stakeholders, which I believe will

help me succeed in this position."

Example:
"I really admire how you have put sustainability at the centre of your business. I first heard about [Company Name] several years ago through your Earth Day awareness campaign. Sustainability is really important to me so I would relish the opportunity to work for a company that values the environmental responsibility as much as I do."

Example:
"I have been working with the same company for a number of years and I believe that my career progression has stalled. I applied for a position here because I wanted a change. I am keen to widen my skill set and I think working here would give me an opportunity to learn new technologies and programming languages. Plus, I would like to work in a new environment and the culture here sounds like it would be a good fit for me. "

An example of how you should not answer this question:
"I just need a job, and I saw that you were hiring, so I thought I'd apply. Honestly, I don't know much about the company or its mission, but I'm willing to work hard."

Don't bash previous employers and/or jobs. Don't just rehash your CV. Your answer can never be, "I need the money" or "I have no other options" or even "I thought I'd apply it looked cool".

Career Goals

Question: What are your long-term career goals?

Similar interview questions:
- *What are your long-term career goals, and how does this position fit into them?*
- *What are your long-term goals?*
- *Where would you like to be in 5 years? 10 years? 20 years?*
- *What is your end goal in your career?*
- *Where do you see yourself progressing in your job?*
- *What do you think will be your last job before retirement?*

Why the interviewer is asking this question:
This question is typically asked towards the end of the interview as a way to wrap up the meeting. It gives the interviewer a final outlook on whether hiring you is the right decision.

The interviewer is asking about your long-term career goals to understand your level of ambition and how your goals align with the company's goals. In other words, how ambitious are you? They want to know if you are a good fit for the company and whether the position you are applying for can help you achieve your goals. It is also used as a reality check to see if you have realistic goals.

The best approach to answering this question:
A possible answer is to express your interest in taking on your boss's role. However, this response requires familiarity with the company's organizational

structure and promotion path.

An example of how to best answer this question
"My long-term career goal is to become a senior software developer in a tech company. I am passionate about coding and technology and have been developing my skills in programming languages such as Java and Python. I believe that this position will help me gain the necessary experience and knowledge to achieve my goal by allowing me to work on various software projects and learn from senior developers. In the short-term, I am looking to specialize in web development and gain more experience in front-end development. Ultimately, I want to continue growing in this field, become proficient in other programming languages, and contribute to building innovative solutions that make a positive impact in people's lives."

An example of how you should not answer this question:
It's important not to convey the message that the job you're applying for is just a stepping stone and that you plan to leave as soon as a better opportunity arises.

* * *

Question: *What are your short-term goals?*

Similar interview questions:
- *What do you plan to accomplish in the next two years?*
- *Where do you see yourself in the near term?*
- *What are your near-term goals?*
- *What do you see as your next position after this one?*

Why the interviewer is asking this question:
The interviewer is asking this question to assess your level of ambition and how well your goals align with the company's mission and vision. They want to know if you have a clear understanding of what you want to achieve in the short term and if you have a plan in place to achieve those goals. A mismatch between your short-term goals and the employer's offerings can be revealed through your response to this question.

The best approach to answering this question:
Be specific and realistic in your goals. Your goals should align with the company's mission and vision and demonstrate your commitment to personal and professional growth. It's also important to mention any skills or knowledge that you plan to acquire in order to achieve your goals.

Your answer should focus on showcasing how you plan to develop yourself to excel in the role for which you are interviewing, with the aim of taking on more responsibilities or progressing to a higher-level position. Make sure to keep your response professional and avoid discussing personal goals.

An example of how to best answer this question
"My short-term goal is to become proficient in using Salesforce, which is an essential tool used in the sales department. I plan to take an online course and attend training sessions offered by the company to achieve this goal within the next six months. I also want to improve my communication skills by taking a public speaking course and attending networking events to build relationships with industry professionals. In addition, I plan to take on more responsibility within my current role, such as leading a project or mentoring new hires, to demonstrate my leadership abilities and contribute to the company's success."

Example:
"I am currently focused on enhancing my core competencies through professional development opportunities and on-the-job experiences. My objective is to excel in my current role and to be fully prepared for future responsibilities and growth within the company. For instance, I recently took charge of a critical project to demonstrate my leadership and problem-solving abilities..."

An example of how you should not answer this question:
Avoid answering this question in a negative or unprofessional way. A response like, "Well, I just want to get out of my current terrible job," could give the impression that you lack motivation and commitment to the potential employer. Instead, focus on discussing your career aspirations and how the position aligns with your goals.

* * *

Question: *Tell me about some of your recent goals and what you did to achieve them*

Similar interview questions:
- *What have you most recently accomplished?*
- *Tell me about a recent project*
- *What objectives do you have in your work and did you complete them?*
- *What plans have you recently completed?*
- *Are you a goal-oriented person?*

Why the interviewer is asking this question:
The interviewer is interested in your goal-setting and achievement process, and wants to know if you are able to plan and execute tasks effectively. They want to see if you are a proactive and motivated individual who takes initiative in your work. Simply put, the interviewer wants to know if you set and achieve goals and how you do it.

The best approach to answering this question:
Consider the question carefully as it is not about your future goals but instead, it's about discussing the recent goals that you have accomplished and how you achieved them. It is a behavioral question, and the most effective way to answer it is by using the STAR (Situation or Task, Action, Results) method. Keep your answer professional and refrain from discussing personal goals.

Provide a clear and concise description of a recent goal you set for yourself and the specific steps you took to achieve it. Highlight any challenges or obstacles you faced and how you overcame them. Use measurable outcomes to show the impact of your actions and highlight the positive results you achieved.

Keep your answer focused on professional goals and achievements, rather than personal hobbies or interests. For instance, it's not relevant to mention accomplishments related to gaming or other leisure activities. Stick to discussing measurable, work-related goals that you've achieved recently.

An example of how to best answer this question:
"During my annual performance planning, I set measurable goals for the following year. In the past year, I had three major goals that I was able to achieve. These goals were focused on [briefly mention the three goals]. Each of these goals required planning, coordination, and consistent effort to achieve. I'm happy to share details on any of them. Which one would you like me to discuss further?"

Example of how you should not answer this question:
"I don't really set goals for myself. I just take things as they come and try to do my best in whatever situation I'm in."

Success

Question: How do you define/measure success?

Similar interview questions:
- *What does success look like to you?*
- *What do you want to accomplish in your first year on the job?*
- *How will you know you are successful in your role?*
- *What will your first performance review say about your results?*
- *What do you think it takes to be successful in this career?*

Why the interviewer is asking this question:
The interviewer wants to understand what drives and motivates you. They are interested in learning about your personal values and how you define success. This could also be an ethical question where the interviewer is interested in how you plan to achieve success and whether you have a plan in place.

The best approach to answering this question:
Define success in a way that aligns with the values of the company you are applying to. It's also important to emphasize that you are proactive in setting and achieving your own goals, while also contributing to the success of the organization.

To impress the interviewer, provide specific examples of your past successes and take them through the steps you personally took to achieve them using the STAR method (Situation or Task, Action, and Results). It's best to focus on a goal that was set for you where you exceeded expectations. By doing so, you can demonstrate your ability to set goals, develop actionable plans, take action, and deliver results.

It's important to be genuine and thoughtful when describing one's definition of success, and to avoid using clichéd or generic responses.

An example of how to best answer this question:
"To me, success is about setting goals and taking steps to achieve them. It's important to me to have a clear sense of purpose and direction, and to work towards making meaningful progress. At the same time, I believe that success is not just about individual achievement, but also about contributing to the success of the team and the organization as a whole.

In my previous role at [previous company], I was successful in achieving [specific accomplishment], but what made me most proud was the impact it had on the team and the company. I was able to [specific action or contribution] which helped the team to reach their goals, and in turn, contributed to the success of the company.

Ultimately, success is about finding a balance between achieving your own goals and making a positive impact on those around you. I am excited about the opportunity to bring this approach to your organization and contribute to its continued success."

The candidate explains success as setting and achieving goals, and contributing to the success of the team and the organization. They also give an example of how they achieved success in their past job and how it helped the team and company. This answer shows the interviewer that the candidate is goal-driven, motivated, and focused on the success of the organization.

Example:
"To me, success means going beyond the expected and delivering exceptional results. Allow me to illustrate this point with an example. My main objective for the past year was to successfully deliver the new accounting system. Although the primary purpose of this upgrade was to modernize our accounting practices, I recognized several manual process steps that could be automated as part of the system upgrade.

After discussing my ideas with the team, we decided to integrate these process steps into the system. As a result, our accounting team now saves a total of 30 to 40 hours each month during month-end closing. By identifying opportunities to improve the system beyond the initial objective, I was able to deliver more value to the organization, which I consider a success."

Example:
"To me, success entails having a rewarding personal life as well as making a positive difference in the world. The quality of my relationships with others, the positive impact I have on my community, and the opportunities I have to learn and grow in my profession are how I define success."

Example of how you should not answer this question:
"I don't believe in measuring success, I just do my best and hope for the best outcome."

* * *

Question: *Describe a situation in which you were successful.*

Similar interview questions:
- *ell me about a time when you did something above-and-beyond.*
- *Give me an example of success in your work.*
- *Have you been successful in the past?*

Why the interviewer is asking this question:
The interviewer is looking for information on your problem-solving skills, decision-making abilities, and ability to work under pressure. They want to know how you define success as well as how you approach and deal with difficult situations.

The best approach to answering this question:
Use the STAR method (Situation or Task, Action, and Results) to provide a specific example of a situation where you were successful. The example should showcase your skills and strengths, highlight the actions you took to achieve success, and demonstrate the positive outcome you achieved.

When answering this question, it's best to provide a work-related example with measurable deliverables that you either achieved on your own or as part of a team, as long as you played a key role in the team's success.

Make sure you're able to provide a detailed explanation of the project or task from start to finish, including your specific role and the actions you took to achieve the outcome.

An example of how to best answer this question
"During my time as a project manager at [previous company], I was assigned to lead a team in delivering a new product launch. We had a tight deadline, and the project was experiencing several unexpected challenges, including supply chain issues and staffing problems.

To address these issues, I took a proactive approach, identifying potential solutions and implementing strategies to mitigate risk. I worked closely with the team to streamline processes, eliminate inefficiencies, and maximize productivity. In addition, I leveraged my interpersonal skills to build strong relationships with stakeholders, including vendors and customers, to ensure everyone was aligned and informed.

As a result of our efforts, we were able to deliver the new product on time and within budget. The product received positive feedback from customers and generated significant revenue for the company. This success not only reinforced my project management skills but also taught me the importance of proactive problem-solving, effective communication, and building strong relationships with stakeholders.

In conclusion, this experience taught me the importance of staying focused and adaptable, especially during challenging times, and how to leverage my strengths and skills to achieve success."

In this example, the candidate uses the STAR method to provide a specific example of a situation where they were successful. They showcase their proactive problem-solving skills, ability to build strong relationships, and the positive outcome they achieved. This response demonstrates to the interviewer that the candidate has the necessary skills and experience to succeed in their role.

Example:
"Let me give you an example of a recent success I had at work. I developed a new productivity system for my personal use, and my boss was impressed by the significant improvements in my productivity. As a result, my boss asked me to lead an adjunct project to roll out the system to other team members.

I was excited about this opportunity and took the lead on the project, working closely with a team of two others. We were able to deliver the system ahead of schedule and within budget. The results have been fantastic – after just three months of use, the system has already increased our team's productivity by 15%.

In fact, the VP of our department is now looking to roll out the system across the company. This project has been a huge success for me personally and for the company as a whole. I'm thrilled to say that the feedback we've received so far has been overwhelmingly positive."

Example of how you should not answer this question:
"I'm successful in everything I do. I have never failed at anything and always achieve my goals. I'm a natural born winner."

Quit Your Previous Job

Question Why do you want to leave your current job?

Similar interview questions:
- Why Did You Leave Your Last Job?

Why the interviewer is asking this question:
The interviewer is asking this question to understand why you are leaving your current job and to determine if you are a good fit for the position and the company culture. They want to make sure you're not leaving because of conflicts, dissatisfaction, or performance issues that could jeopardize your performance in the new job.

The best approach to answering this question:
Whether you are currently unemployed, have left your previous job, or are in the process of searching for a new one while still employed, it's crucial to be honest when answering this question. If you were fired, laid off, or resigned, be straightforward and explain the situation clearly.

It's important to avoid negativity when discussing your current or previous employers as it can make you come across as bitter or petty.

Focus your response on seeking a company with cultural dynamics that better suit you, versus blaming the company for the lack of fit.

Focus less on the reason for leaving and more on the why you wanted to move to this new company. For example, you can say that you admire the company's culture, missions and the projects. You can simply say that you were looking for a more challenging role and also better opportunities for career growth.

An example of how to best answer this question:
If you're pursuing a new job due to a recent relocation to a different city or country, or if you're proactively seeking new opportunities because your current company is unstable and possibly downsizing, it's essential to mention these reasons upfront. However, be sure to avoid complaining about the situation.

Say it was not a good fit:
Your company has gone through a lot of organizational changes, has hired new management, and has an evolving corporate culture and strategy, and the company is no longer a good fit for you.

For Growth:
Say that you left their previous job to pursue new challenges or opportunities for growth and development. You can explain that you are seeking a better work-life balance, or that you are looking for a company that aligned more closely with your values and career goals.

Define what positive things you desire in your next job. Examples: supportive co-workers, a respectful community, a trusted manager, and a chance for promotion based on merit.

You can probably say there was no opportunity in your previous job for growth in your career.

You can say that you felt your talent is underutilised so you are looking to move to a company where you can grow and develop in your career. You can say, "I'm looking for an environment that unleashes my full potential."

Tell them that you are looking for a greater challenge, new growth opportunities. I think this is a politically correct answer.

Say you have completed the project:
"I successfully completed the term of my contract and delivered my project on time despite xyz roadblocks."

Tell the truth:
"Because my manager was a micromanaging."
"Truth is I got in a fight with my previous boss, turns out he promoted a girl he was seeing"

An example of how you should not answer this question:
"I hate my current job. My boss is a nightmare, and I can't stand working there anymore. I just need to get out of there as soon as possible."

This type of answer is negative, unprofessional, and might raise concerns about your attitude and work ethic. This question is not a prompt for you to vent your anger at your ex-employer. Speaking ill of your ex-employer might hurt your chance because your new company do not want whiners or complainers. So do not badmouth your last your job or your previous boss.

* * *

Question: *Why were you fired?*

Similar interview questions:
- *Why were you let go?*

Why the interviewer is asking this question:
The interviewer is asking this question to understand the circumstances surrounding your termination and to gauge your level of self-awareness, accountability, and ability to learn from past mistakes. They want to ensure that you can handle difficult situations professionally and that the reasons for your dismissal will not be a recurring issue in your new role.

The best approach to answering this question:
Be honest: If you were truly fired, you need to be prepared to answer this question. Explain the reason behind your dismissal truthfully, without getting too emotional or defensive. If it was a retrenchment, or the company was downsizing, say so. If you were fired due to your employer's unhappiness with you, say so.

Take responsibility: Acknowledge your part in the situation and show that you understand the reasons for your termination. Explain how you requested to sit down and chat with them to understand how you can avoid such situations in the future.

Demonstrate growth: Explain what you've learned from the experience and the steps you've taken to improve yourself and avoid similar situations in the future. You want to show how you have developed and grown from that incident.

Stay positive: Maintain a positive attitude, focusing on your enthusiasm for the new role and your commitment to being a valuable team member. Explain that you are willing to approach your new job's tasks with an open and positive mindset.

An example of how to best answer this question:
"In my previous role, I was let go due to a disagreement with my manager regarding a project's direction. I take responsibility for my part in the situation, and in hindsight, I could have communicated my concerns more effectively. Since then, I've taken a course on conflict resolution and improved my communication skills. I've learned from this experience, and I am eager to apply these lessons and contribute positively to your company."

An example of how you should not answer this question:
"I was fired because my boss was an idiot who didn't know what they were doing. They never listened to my ideas, and when things went wrong, they blamed me. Honestly, it's their loss, and I'm just glad to be done with that place."

Question: *What did you like or dislike about your previous job?*

Similar interview questions:
- *Tell me about what worked well and what did not work well in your prior role.*
- *What were the best and worst things about your last employer?*
- *How would you describe the highlights and lowlights of your current work life?*

- *Give me an example of how you supported what you liked or tried to change what you didn't like in your last job.*

Why the interviewer is asking this question:
The interviewer wants to know what you liked and didn't like about your previous job to understand your work preferences, values, and motivations. They aim to evaluate if the current job is suitable for you and whether you would be content in the role. Based on your answer, the interviewer can identify any potential concerns or issues.

The best approach to answering this question:
If there were aspects of the job that you didn't like, try to frame them in a constructive way and focus on how you learned from those experiences or how they helped you grow.

An example of how to best answer this question:
"I really enjoyed the team collaboration and the opportunity to work on diverse projects in my previous role. However, I found that I wasn't as fulfilled in the administrative tasks and paperwork that were required. But, I did learn the importance of time management and attention to detail, which I believe will be valuable in this new role."

Example:
"I really enjoyed the opportunities for professional development in my previous job, particularly the mentoring program that helped me develop new skills and take on more challenging projects. However, I did find that the company culture was very hierarchical, and there wasn't as much collaboration among

different teams as I would have liked. That's why I'm excited about this opportunity with your company, as I've heard great things about your commitment to employee development and collaboration across departments."

An example of how you should not answer this question:
"I hated my last job. My boss was a micromanager who never gave me the freedom to take initiative, and my co-workers were all backstabbers who only cared about advancing their own careers. I'm so glad to be out of there."

"Well, I don't usually like to gripe, but there were several things wrong with my last job, which is why I'm no longer there. They had really strict delivery schedules, which drove me crazy, because I wanted to just get stuff done on my own time and schedule without some arbitrary deadline hanging over me…"

Gaps

Question: *Why was there a gap in your employment?*

Why the interviewer is asking this question:
They want to ensure that you are a reliable candidate who will be dedicated to the role and company.

The best approach to answering this question:
Be direct about the gap you experienced; was it for a good cause (charity, volunteer work, taking care of your young child or elderly parents), or other personal activities like furthering your education or traveling across the world? If your gap was simply because you couldn't find a job, explain to the interviewer why this was the case – maybe you were shifting industries and wanted to learn the ropes from mentors before jumping onboard full time, or you just needed a break.

Emphasize the positive: Highlight any personal growth, skills, or experiences gained during that time, and explain how they could be beneficial to the role.

Show commitment: Reassure the interviewer that you are now focused on your career and dedicated to the role you're applying for.

An example of how to best answer this question:
"During the gap in my employment, I took time off to care for my elderly parents. Although it was a challenging time, it helped me develop strong problem-solving and time management skills, which I believe will be valuable in this role. I also used the time to further my education by taking online courses in [relevant subject]. I am now fully committed to my

career and excited about the opportunity to contribute to your company."

An example of how you should not answer this question:

"I didn't do anything to improve my skills or learn anything new. I just hung out with my friends and played video games because I couldn't find a job. But everyone needs a break from time to time."

This answer does not demonstrate any initiative, work ethic, or commitment to personal or professional growth, which could be a red flag for the interviewer.

Ambition

Question: What are you looking for in your next job?

Why the interviewer is asking this question:
The interviewer wants to know what you value in a job and what motivates you. This question helps the interviewer determine if the company can provide the kind of work environment, benefits, and job responsibilities that align with your goals and values. It also helps them understand if you have thought carefully about what you want and if you are serious about pursuing this job opportunity.

The best approach to answering this question:
You can focus on the aspects of your previous job that you enjoyed and would like to have in your next job, and also mention any areas for growth and learning that you are interested in.

Focus on the little things that matter, such as your disinterest in office gossip and politics. Emphasize your preference for a positive work environment where everyone works towards a common goal. In addition, talk about your desire to explore opportunities while still being able to maintain a work-life balance and spend quality time with your family.

Good answers will focus on exploring other opportunities and seeking career progression – things that your current or previous job might not be able to provide due to the size of the company, for instance.

An example of how to best answer this question:
"I am looking for a job that challenges me and allows

me to continue growing my skills. In my previous job, I enjoyed collaborating with a team and being involved in projects from start to finish. I'm also interested in finding a job that provides opportunities for professional development and learning. After researching your company, I believe this role aligns with my career goals and would allow me to contribute to a dynamic team."

An example of how you should not answer this question
"I just want a job that pays well and has good benefits. I didn't really like my last job and just want something different."

It's important not to express a preference for working at a larger company like Google when applying for a position at a small, family-run business with a desk-bound job.

Some answers that will raise red flags include: a higher salary, a more flexible working schedule, or even the need for an easy job.

* * *

Question: *Would you rather work with information or with people?*

Similar interview questions:
- *Are you a people person?*
- *Do you enjoy working with things or with people?*
- *Would you rather be heads-down in the data or meeting with people all day?*
- *What part of your job do you enjoy the most?*

Why the interviewer is asking this question:
The interviewer is attempting to determine the candidate's preferred balance of working with people, data, and/or things. Most jobs include some combination of these three elements, but the degree of combination varies by job. The response can also reveal the candidate's communication style and ability to work with a variety of tasks and personalities.

The best approach to answering this question:
Most jobs require a balance of two or three elements. So avoid choosing one option over the other. Instead emphasize the importance of balancing both working with information and working with people in the workplace. Highlight your ability to handle different aspects of the job and work effectively in a variety of situations.

An example of how to best answer this question
"I believe that both information and people are important in any job. While I enjoy working with information and analyzing data, I also understand the value of collaboration and building strong

relationships with co-workers and clients. Finding a balance between the two is key to achieving success in any role."

Example:
"In my current job, there is a primary focus on working with information, but there is also a significant people element involved. Over time, I have noticed a gradual shift in emphasis from information toward people as I have progressed in my career. I believe it's important to excel at both aspects, as there are individuals in my profession who may excel at dealing with information but may lack people skills. Recently, I was promoted due to my ability to work effectively with both information and people, which enabled me to make significant contributions to my team's success."

An example of how you should not answer this question:
"I have a strong preference for working with information. In fact, some of my co-workers have even jokingly referred to me as a "closet coder," implying that I'm most productive when left to work independently on coding projects. I tend to get easily distracted and prefer to minimize interruptions, so I often wear earbuds with loud music to signal to others that I am focused on my work."

* * *

Question What do you hope to achieve in this role?

Why the interviewer is asking this question:
The interviewer wants to know about your goals and plans to see if they match the company's objectives. They also want to know if you fully understand the job responsibilities and have a strategy for succeeding in the role.

The best approach to answering this question:
Show that you understand the job duties and explain how your skills and experience make you a good fit for the role. Align your career goals with the company's objectives and emphasize how you plan to contribute to the company's success using your skills and experience.

An example of how to best answer this question:
"I am excited about the opportunity to work in this position and contribute to the company's success. My main goal is to produce high-quality work while exceeding expectations in all aspects of the job. I hope to form strong bonds with my co-workers and learn from their experiences while also sharing my own abilities and knowledge. I'd also like to take on more responsibilities and advance within the company."

An example of how you should not answer this question
"I'm not really sure what I hope to achieve in this role. I just need a job right now, and this one seemed like a good fit. I hope to learn more about the job responsibilities as I go along."

Ideal Work Environment

Question: Describe your ideal work environment.

Why the interviewer is asking this question:
The interviewer is asking this question to understand your work style and preferences to see if they align with the company's culture and environment. This information can help the interviewer determine if you would be a good fit for the team and the company.

The best approach to answering this question:
Be honest and provide a response that aligns with the company's culture and environment. Do some research on the company culture and work environment before the interview to ensure your answer is relevant and accurate.

Examples of ideal work environment are: an environment that fosters collaboration, creativity, and autonomy. You value having a supportive and inclusive team culture, flexible work arrangements, and opportunities for professional development and growth.

Avoid describing an ideal work environment that is unrealistic given the nature of the job or company culture.

An example of how to best answer this question:
"A work environment that values collaboration and teamwork is ideal for me. I like having the freedom to work independently while also being able to rely on my colleagues for support and guidance. I did some research on this company and talked to some

employees, and it seems that collaboration and teamwork are highly valued here, which is very exciting for me as it aligns with my work style."

An example of how you should not answer this question
"I don't really have an ideal work environment. I can work anywhere as long as I have a computer and an internet connection. I don't really care about the company culture or the people I work with as long as I get my work done."

Question: What would make this job fulfilling for you?

Why the interviewer is asking this question:
The interviewer is asking this question to understand what motivates you and what you value in a job. This information can help them assess whether you will be a good fit for the position and the company culture.

The best approach to answering this question:
Most candidates, when asked this question, will start to fantasize about what would make them happy. They give answers in terms of outcomes to them: Money. Vacations. Xmas bonus. Benefits.

The best approach is to be honest and specific about what you find fulfilling in a job. It's important to focus on what you can contribute to the company rather than just what the company can do for you. You can talk about how the job aligns with your career goals and how you can see yourself growing and developing within the role.

An example of how to best answer this question:
"I feel happy when I can create a positive impact in my work. The opportunity to work on projects that can make a difference for our clients and contribute to the success of the company excites me in this role. I like to work in a team where everyone is working towards a common goal. I think this company's culture and values align with mine, and I believe I can succeed here and continue to learn and grow. "

Example:
"I just want to serve the customers and make this business run like a well-oiled machine. I know if I do that, things will go well with me. If I make the boss's job easier, please the customers, and become a highly-productive employee, then the rewards will appear."

An example of how you should not answer this question:
"I just want a job that pays well and has good benefits. I don't care about what the job entails as long as I'm making money. I'm not particular about the work environment as long as it's not too stressful."

Questions for interviewers

Question: Do you have any questions for me?

Why the interviewer is asking this question:
The interviewer is asking this question to give you the opportunity to clarify any doubts or concerns you may have about the job or the company. It also shows your interest in the job and your willingness to learn more. This is your chance to assess the organization and whether you really want to work there. Determine if this opportunity is right for you.

The best approach to answering this question:
It is NOT good not to ask questions when prompted to. Here's why. The interviewer is testing you to see if you are curious or interested in the company or your work enough to want to find out more. Show your interest by asking questions.

Prepare a few thoughtful and relevant questions in advance. Avoid asking questions that can easily be found on the company's website or in job descriptions. The questions you ask should demonstrate your knowledge of the company and your interest in the job. Make sure your questions are open-ended and give the interviewer a chance to elaborate on their answer.

What meaningful questions can you ask the interviewer? Here are some suggestions:
- After going through my CV and discussing the job with me, do you have any concerns with me working in this company and for this position?

- Do you have any reservation about my skills or experience?
- What are the roles and responsibilities of this position?
- If I will be hired, what are the first three things you would want me to accomplish first?
- How will my performance be measured?
- Will there be any training provided?
- Are there certain company policies here that I should be aware of prior to starting my role?
- How soon can I be informed of the outcome of the interview? / When can I possibly hear back from you regarding the outcome of the interview?

An example of how to best answer this question:
I think the most important question is this: "Is there any reason you wouldn't offer me this position?"

If the answer is no, you've got the job. If the answer is yes then you can clear their doubts, handle any objections or address any concerns they have.

An example of how you should not answer this question
"No, I don't have any questions. I think you've already answered everything I need to know."

Do not repeat anything that has already been mentioned. Clarify if you must but refrain from asking things that have already been brought up in the job advertisement or towards the beginning of the interview. It might show your lack of attentiveness towards them.

Interpersonal and Communication Questions:

These questions focus on your ability to work well with others and communicate effectively.

Conflict Management and Resolution

Question: Have you ever had a conflict with a boss/co-worker/team member? How was it resolved?

Similar interview questions:
- *How do you handle conflict with co-worker's or team members?*
- *How do you handle conflict in the workplace?*
- *What is your experience with conflict resolution?*
- *How are you at dealing with conflict?*
- *What do you do when you disagree with others?*
- *Do you open up or close down in conflict situations?*
- *How do you handle disagreements?*
- *Do you handle conflict well?*
- *Tell me about a time where you had a disagreement with your boss or co-worker.*
- *If you see someone doing something clearly wrong at work, would you confront that person or ignore it?*
- *How do you handle it when someone requests that you do something you don't want to do?*
- *Do you ever get into arguments with others?*

Why the interviewer is asking this question:
The interviewer is assessing your ability to work collaboratively with others., emotional intelligence, and conflict resolution skills. They want to see if you are able to handle difficult situations and maintain a positive working relationship.

The best approach to answering this question:
The best approach to answering this question is to be honest and provide a specific example of a conflict you had, how you handled the situation, and what the outcome was. It's important to focus on how you resolved the conflict in a professional and respectful manner.

You should emphasize your ability to remain calm and composed, actively listen to the other person's perspective, and find a mutually agreeable solution.

It's important to avoid placing blame or speaking negatively about others when discussing conflicts, and instead focus on the positive aspects of the experience and how it helped you develop their conflict resolution skills.

An example of how to best answer this question:
Here's an example of how to best answer this question:

"I have had a conflict with a boss in the past, but I was able to resolve it in a professional and respectful manner. The conflict arose when I was working on a project and my boss had a different vision for how it should be executed. We had a disagreement about the approach, which led to tension and frustration on both sides.

To resolve the conflict, I requested a one-on-one meeting with my boss to discuss our different perspectives. During the meeting, I listened to my boss's concerns and tried to understand their perspective. I then explained my own perspective and suggested a compromise that would address both of our concerns.

Through this open and respectful dialogue, we were able to reach an agreement that satisfied both of us. We were able to complete the project successfully, and our working relationship remained positive and productive.

I believe that conflicts are an inevitable part of any workplace, but it's important to handle them professionally and with respect for everyone involved. I think that open communication and a willingness to listen to different perspectives is key to resolving conflicts and maintaining positive working relationships."

In this example, The candidate shares a specific conflict they had with their boss, and how they handled it professionally. They emphasize the importance of open communication and being willing to listen to others' perspectives to resolve conflicts effectively.

Example:
For example, you could say that you once had a disagreement with a colleague over how to approach

a project, and that you scheduled a meeting to discuss the issue in a respectful and open manner. You could explain that you listened carefully to your colleague's concerns and ideas, and shared your own perspective in a clear and respectful way. You could also describe how you worked collaboratively with your colleague to find a solution that incorporated both perspectives and achieved the project goals.

An example of how you should not answer this question:
"Well, conflicts are the main reason I'm leaving my current job. I cannot handle the constant stress and tension around me. I've tried using earbuds to drown out the noise, but people still yell at me and it only adds to my frustration. So, I usually just walk away. That's why I'm here, looking for a new opportunity."

Pressure/Stress Management

Question: *Do you handle pressure well?*

Similar interview questions:
- *How do you react when under pressure?*
- *How are you with making deadlines?*
- *How do you respond when you need to deliver something without having enough time to do the job correctly?*
- *How do you respond to stress?*

Why the interviewer is asking this question:
The interviewer is asking this question to understand how well you can handle stress and pressure in the workplace. This is important because many jobs come with high levels of stress, and employers want to know that you can handle the demands of the job without cracking under pressure.

This question also indicates that the job may involve a significant amount of pressure or stress, which could be a reason why previous candidates may not have performed well. The interviewer is looking for your personal evaluation of how you manage pressure and stress in order to determine if you are a good fit for the position.

The best approach to answering this question:
Provide a specific example of a time when you had to handle a stressful situation at work and explain how you dealt with it. You should also discuss any techniques you use to manage stress and pressure in the workplace.

For example, provide a concrete example of a time when you had to perform under pressure or meet a tight deadline and were able to deliver successfully. Choose an example where you not only met the deadline, but also exceeded expectations with the quality of your work or the results achieved. Use the STAR (Situation, Task, Action, Result) method to give a detailed account of the situation and the actions you took to accomplish the task.

An example of how to best answer this question
"I do well under pressure. Actually, I thrive under pressure because it pushes me to work harder and smarter. For example, in my previous job as a project manager, we were running late for a major deadline. This placed a lot of pressure on the team to complete everything on time. I called a team meeting to discuss the situation, and we devised a strategy to divide the work into smaller, more manageable tasks. We also delegated tasks and established regular check-ins to ensure that everyone was on track. We were able to meet the deadline with plenty of time to spare, and the project was a huge success as a result."

Example:
"I believe I handle pressure well, and I can provide an example to illustrate this. Our team was recently tasked with adding a new feature to our product that wasn't included in the original release schedule. As the team lead, it was my responsibility to ensure that we could deliver the updated product on time and without any bugs. To accomplish this, I reorganized the team's priorities and created a detailed plan for the new feature's implementation. We worked longer hours and weekends to make up for lost time, and we

communicated regularly to ensure everyone was on the same page. Thanks to our efforts, we not only met the deadline but also exceeded the expectations of management by delivering a high-quality product that received positive feedback from customers."

An example of how you should not answer this question:
"I absolutely cannot handle pressure at all. Whenever there's a deadline or a difficult situation, I just shut down and can't focus on anything. I usually end up making mistakes and underperforming. That's just how I am."

Persuasion

Question Describe a time when you had to persuade someone to see things your way.

Why the interviewer is asking this question:
The interviewer is asking this question to assess the candidate's communication skills, ability to influence and persuade others, and how they handle conflict or differences of opinion.

The best approach to answering this question:
1. Start with a specific situation: Begin your response by briefly describing the situation you were in, including the context and the people involved.

2. Explain the challenge: Clearly explain the challenge you faced and why it was important to persuade the other person to see things your way.

3. Describe your approach: Explain the approach you took to persuade the person. Describe any strategies or techniques you used, such as building rapport, presenting facts and evidence, or using storytelling.

4. Highlight the results: Finally, highlight the positive outcome that resulted from your efforts to persuade the other person. Explain how your ability to persuade and influence helped you achieve a successful outcome.

An example of how to best answer this question:
"In my previous role, I worked on a project with a team member who had a different approach to problem-solving. We were tasked with finding a solution to a

complex issue, and I believed that my approach would be the most effective. However, my colleague had a different opinion and was resistant to my ideas. To persuade them to see things my way, I started by building rapport and acknowledging their perspective.

I presented them with the facts and data I had gathered to support my approach and explained how it would lead to the best outcome for the project. I also used examples from previous successful projects to demonstrate how my approach had worked in the past. In the end, my colleague agreed to my approach, and we were able to successfully resolve the issue and deliver the project on time."

An example of how you should not answer this question
"I never had to persuade someone to see things my way because everyone always agreed with me. I'm very convincing and always have the best ideas."

Leadership

Question: What is your leadership/management style?

Why the interviewer is asking this question:
The interviewer wants to know your leadership and management style if you're applying for a managerial position. They want to learn how you motivate and work with your team to achieve goals. Additionally, the interviewer wants to determine if you have the skills required to lead and manage a team successfully.

The best approach to answering this question:
Start by outlining the values and principles that guide your leadership style, and then give examples of how you have applied them in previous roles. Be sure to focus on results achieved and how you motivated your team to accomplish them.

You could say that your management style is collaborative and participatory, where you seek input and feedback from team members to make decisions and prioritize tasks. You could explain that you provide clear expectations and goals, and regularly check in with the team to ensure that everyone is on track. You could also describe how you provide constructive feedback and recognition to the team members, and support their professional development and growth.

An example of how to best answer this question:
"I believe in a participative leadership style where I involve my team members in decision-making and

goal-setting. I set clear expectations and provide regular feedback to ensure that everyone is on track. In my previous role as a project manager, I successfully led a team of 10 people to complete a project ahead of schedule by empowering them to take ownership of their work and collaborating closely with them throughout the process."

An example of how you should not answer this question:
"I don't really have a management style. I just let my team do what they want as long as they meet their targets."

* * *

Question: What qualities do you think are important for a leader to possess?

Similar interview questions:
- *What qualities do you feel a successful manager should have?*
- *Tell me about your best boss.*
- *Did you have a boss you liked working with in the past?*
- *What is the best way to manage you as an employee?*

Why the interviewer is asking this question:
The interviewer wants to know what you value in a leader and how you would approach leadership if given the opportunity. They want to know if your values and beliefs align with the company's culture and values. The interviewer is probing your work style.

The best approach to answering this question:
Highlights qualities you believe are essential for effective leadership. Choose qualities that are relevant to the job you are applying for and to provide specific examples or scenarios that demonstrate these qualities.

Examples of leadership qualities are effective communication, strong emotional intelligence, the ability to inspire and motivate others, and a commitment to integrity and ethics.

An example of how to best answer this question
"A good leader should be honest, communicate effectively, and lead by example. They must motivate

their team to achieve their goals and provide constructive feedback. In addition, a good leader should be quick to address any problems that arise. Building strong relationships with team members and creating a positive work environment are qualities of the best leaders, in my opinion."

Example:
"In my opinion, a great manager is someone who can give the team a clear view of the big picture. They should help us understand where we're heading and how our work fits into the overall direction of the company. But, they should also be focused on delivering results.

I had a manager not too long ago who did an amazing job of keeping our team on track with delivering results that aligned with a recent change in corporate direction. It was pretty impressive to see how they were able to keep us all on the same page and working together towards the same goal."

Team Player

Question: How do you build relationships with team members or clients?

Why the interviewer is asking this question:
The interviewer is likely asking this question to determine how well you can work with others and build positive relationships in a professional setting. This is an important skill in many industries, as it can affect teamwork, productivity, and overall success in achieving business goals.

The best approach to answering this question:
Provide specific examples of how you have built successful relationships with team members or clients in the past. Share your strategies for building trust and rapport, such as active listening, clear communication, and a collaborative approach. Highlight your ability to adapt to different communication styles and work effectively with people from diverse backgrounds. Emphasis on the importance of communication, empathy, and trust.

An example of how to best answer this question:
"I believe that building strong relationships is crucial for any successful project. In my previous roles, I've found that taking the time to get to know my team members or clients on a personal level helped establish trust and open lines of communication. I always make sure to actively listen to their concerns and ideas, and collaborate with them on ways to achieve our goals together.

For instance, I led a project where I worked closely with a client who had some difficult demands. I took the time to understand their needs and concerns, and we were able to establish a rapport that allowed us to work collaboratively towards a successful outcome. It's all about communication, empathy, and building trust with people from diverse backgrounds, and adapting to their communication styles."

An example of how you should not answer this question:
"I don't really focus on building relationships with team members or clients. I prefer to just do my work and let others do theirs. I find that building relationships can be a distraction from getting things done."

* * *

Question: Are you a team player?

Similar interview questions:
- *Do you like working in a team?*
- *Are you better on a team or working by yourself?*
- *Tell me about a team project and your contribution.*

Why the interviewer is asking this question:
The interviewer is asking about your ability to work as part of a team because most jobs require collaboration with others. They want to know if you have experience working in a team environment, how well you will perform and how you contribute to the success of the team.

One of the most difficult aspects of interviewing is understanding what the candidate accomplished vs. what the candidate's team accomplished. And did the team accomplish the results because of the candidate or in spite of the candidate. It's common for a high performing team to have one (or two or three) team members who are not producing like the other members of the team. So a good interviewer will seek to probe into your specific role, interaction within the team and contributions to the results.

The best approach to answering this question:
Give an example of how you have worked in a positive way with your team. For managers, this can take on a second dimension of managing a team. For most, however, it should be focused on how we interact with and communicate with others at a peer level on a work team and the results achieved, making note of outstanding contributions to the team. Final note: in

spite of the temptation, do not answer with sports analogies or sports cliches.

Here's an example of how to best answer this question:
"I am absolutely a team player. In fact, I believe that working effectively as part of a team is crucial for success in any job. In my previous position at [previous company], I was part of a project team that was tasked with [describe project goal]. My role on the team was to [describe your specific responsibilities]. We faced some challenges during the project, including [describe challenges], but we were able to work together and overcome them. I contributed by [describe specific actions you took to support the team]. In the end, we were able to [describe successful project outcome and how it benefited the team or company].

I believe that my ability to work effectively as part of a team comes from my willingness to communicate openly and honestly with my team members, as well as my ability to listen and be open to feedback. I think it's important to build trust and respect within a team so that everyone feels comfortable contributing their ideas and suggestions."

In this example, the candidate provides a specific example of a time when they worked effectively as part of a team. They highlight their role on the team, the challenges they faced, and the positive outcome that was achieved. In addition, they explain how they contributed to the success of the team and highlight the qualities that make them a good team player, such as communication and openness to feedback.

Communication

Question: Describe a time when you had to communicate a complex idea to someone with no technical knowledge.

Why the interviewer is asking this question:
The interviewer is asking this question to assess your ability to communicate complex ideas effectively to people who have no technical knowledge. This skill is crucial in many industries where technical information needs to be presented to non-technical stakeholders.

The best approach to answering this question:
The best approach is to use the STAR method:
Situation: Describe the situation or project where you had to communicate a complex idea to someone with no technical knowledge.
Task: Explain the technical idea and the challenges you faced in communicating it effectively to the person.
Action: Describe the steps you took to break down the complex idea into simple terms and how you made sure the person understood it.
Result: Explain the outcome of your communication and how your approach made a difference.

An example of how to best answer this question:
"During my previous job, I was working on a project that involved developing a software application. I had to communicate the technical details of the project to the client who had no technical knowledge. I used analogies and simple language to explain the technical concepts in a way that the client could easily

understand. I also provided visual aids such as diagrams and charts to simplify the process. By the end of our conversation, the client was able to grasp the technical details and provided positive feedback on my ability to communicate complex ideas effectively."

An example of how you should not answer this question:
"I have never had to communicate a complex idea to someone with no technical knowledge."

Criticism

Question: How do you handle criticism?

Why the interviewer is asking this question:
The interviewer wants to know how you handle feedback and criticism and if you are open to learning from your mistakes.

The best approach to answering this question:
To answer this question, you should show that you can handle criticism professionally and constructively. Firstly, acknowledge that criticism is a part of learning and that you welcome feedback. Secondly, give an example of when you received criticism and explain how you responded to it and how it helped you improve your work. Lastly, emphasize that you value feedback as an opportunity to grow and learn.

An example of how to best answer this question:
"I think that accepting criticism is necessary for growth in any profession, and I'm always open to feedback. For instance, during a project in my previous job, a team member suggested some areas where I could improve my work. I appreciated their input, and we worked together to find solutions to enhance my work. As a result, our team accomplished our objectives. I believe that taking feedback is a chance for progress, and I'm determined to learn from my errors."

An example of how you should not answer this question:
"I don't really handle criticism very well. It can be frustrating and demotivating, especially if it's not constructive. I prefer to work independently, so I don't have to worry about receiving criticism from others."

Teamwork

Question: Give me an example of a time when you had to work with a team to achieve a goal.

Why the interviewer is asking this question:
The interviewer wants to see if you're a team player and can work well with others towards a shared objective. They're interested in hearing about how you communicate with your teammates, deal with any conflicts that may arise, and what you do to help the team achieve its goals.

The best approach to answering this question:
The best approach is to use the STAR method (Situation, Task, Action, Result) to provide a specific and detailed example of a time when you worked successfully with a team to achieve a goal. Be sure to highlight your role in the team, how you communicated with others, and how you contributed to the team's success.

An example of how to best answer this question:
Situation: At my previous job, I was part of a team responsible for launching a new product.
Task: Our goal was to launch the product within a tight deadline and with a limited budget.
Action: To achieve this goal, we set up weekly meetings to discuss our progress, identify potential roadblocks, and assign tasks to team members. I took the lead on coordinating with the marketing team to create a promotional campaign for the product launch. I also offered to help team members who were struggling with their tasks.

Result: Our team was able to launch the product on time and within budget, and it was very successful in the market. We received positive feedback from our customers, and the product sales exceeded our expectations.

An example of how you should not answer this question:
"I have always been a team player and have never faced any issues while working in a team. I have always been able to work well with my team members and have always contributed to achieving team goals."

This type of answer does not provide a specific example and does not demonstrate your ability to work effectively with others.

Giving Feedback

Question: Describe a time when you had to give difficult feedback to a team member.

Similar interview questions:
- *How would you handle a situation where a co-worker was not meeting expectations?*

Why the interviewer is asking this question:
The question aims to understand the candidate's ability to manage performance issues with their colleagues in a constructive and professional manner.

The best approach to answering this question:
When answering this question, a candidate should describe specific steps they would take to address the situation, such as providing feedback, setting clear expectations, and working collaboratively with the co-worker to develop a plan for improvement. The candidate should also explain how they would maintain a positive and respectful relationship with their colleague throughout the process.

An example of how to best answer this question:
"If a co-worker expressed concerns about their work, I would first speak with them about it. I would provide feedback on areas where they could improve and collaborate with them to develop a strategy for success. We would set clear expectations and locate any resources they might require to achieve their objectives."

An example of how you should not answer this question:

"I have always been a team player and have never faced any issues while working in a team. I have always been able to work well with my team members and have always contributed to achieving team goals."

Setting Priority

Question: How do you prioritize your work?

Why the interviewer is asking this question:
The question aims to understand the candidate's ability to manage their workload effectively and efficiently.

The best approach to answering this question:
Describe specific strategies to prioritize tasks, such as setting goals, breaking down projects into smaller tasks, and identifying urgent and important tasks. You can also explain how you manage competing priorities and communicate with team members and stakeholders to ensure that deadlines are met.

An example of how to best answer this question:
You could say that you use the Eisenhower matrix to prioritize tasks, which involves categorizing tasks into four categories based on their urgency and importance. You could also explain that you regularly review their tasks and adjust their priorities as needed, while also communicating proactively with team members to ensure that everyone is on the same page.

An example of how you should not answer this question:
Do not say that you don't prioritize your work and just do everything at once.

Work-life Balance

Question: What are your thoughts on work-life balance?

Why the interviewer is asking this question:
The question aims to understand the candidate's perspective on the importance of balancing work and personal life. The employer wants to know if you are able to manage your workload while still maintaining a healthy work-life balance. It also helps them to see if your values align with the company's culture and policies.

The best approach to answering this question:
Avoid extreme answers and maintain a balanced approach. Show that you can prioritize your work and maintain a healthy lifestyle. Provide examples of how you have managed your workload and achieved a work-life balance in your previous roles. Research the company's culture and policies regarding work-life balance and incorporate that into your answer.

An example of how to best answer this question:
"I believe that maintaining a healthy work-life balance is crucial for achieving job satisfaction and productivity. I prioritize my workload by setting achievable goals and timelines, and I ensure that I maintain a healthy lifestyle outside of work. For example, I make time for exercise, hobbies, and spending time with my family and friends. I also research the company's culture and policies regarding work-life balance and strive to align my values with theirs. I believe that a good work-life balance allows me to perform better in my role and contributes to the

overall success of the team."

An example of how you should not answer this question:
"I don't really care about work-life balance. I just work until the job is done. If that means working long hours and sacrificing my personal life, then so be it. I believe that hard work and dedication are more important than maintaining a work-life balance."

Teamwork

Question: What is your experience with teamwork?

Why the interviewer is asking this question:
The interviewer wants to know if you are good at working with others to achieve common goals. They want to see if you can communicate well and fit in with the company culture. Teamwork is important in most workplaces.

The best approach to answering this question:
Provide specific examples of times when you worked well with others in a team setting, highlighting your contribution and achievements. It is also essential to describe your communication style, your willingness to listen to others' opinions and ideas, and your ability to resolve conflicts constructively.

An example of how to best answer this question:
"I have extensive experience working in teams, and I believe that collaboration is essential to achieving success. In my previous job, I worked as part of a cross-functional team to develop a new product, and I was responsible for coordinating with the sales and marketing teams. I organized regular meetings, listened to their feedback, and incorporated their suggestions into the project. Through open communication and teamwork, we were able to launch the product ahead of schedule and exceed our sales target by 20%. I believe in sharing responsibilities, setting clear expectations, and working together to achieve our common goals."

An example of how you should not answer this question:

"I prefer working alone and find it easier to complete tasks independently. I'm not much of a people person and have had conflicts with team members in the past, which have affected my productivity. However, if I have to work in a team, I usually let others take the lead, and I follow their instructions."

Technical and industry-specific questions

These questions aim to understand your knowledge of specific technical or industry-related topics.

Company

Question: What do you know about our company?

Similar interview questions:
- *Do you understand the different parts of our company?*
- *When did you first learn about our company?*
- *What can you tell me about our company?*
- *Do you understand our company's market positioning?*

Why the interviewer is asking this question:
The interviewer is asking this question to gauge your level of interest in the company and the position for which you are interviewing. It also shows that you have done your research and have an understanding of the company's mission, values, and culture.

The best approach to answering this question:
Before the interview, research the company thoroughly. Look for information on the company's history, products or services, mission statement, recent news, and any notable achievements. This information can be gathered from the company's website, social media accounts, press releases, and news articles.

When answering the question, be concise and highlight the most important and relevant information. Connect the company's mission and values with your skills and experience to demonstrate your fit for the position. Ask thoughtful questions to show your interest and engage with the interviewer.

It's important to demonstrate a genuine interest and enthusiasm for the company and the industry. You don't have to know everything about the company. Just be prepared to answer why you want to work there. Maybe you really like the product they are selling. Maybe you read that they work with a lot of charities and you appreciate how much they give back to the community. Maybe you know someone that works there and were told that they have a great work culture.

An example of how to best answer this question:
"So I looked up your company online and I got to say, I'm pretty impressed with how you guys come up with new solutions to industry problems. It's also really cool to see that you're big on diversity and inclusion, which is totally in line with my own values. And congrats on that award you recently won for your latest product - it really shows that your team knows how to put in the hard work! I'm excited about the opportunity to bring my skills and experience to such an innovative company like yours."

An example of how you should not answer this question:
"I don't know much about your company, to be honest. I just applied to this position because I need a job. Can you tell me a bit more about what you do?"

* * *

Question: *Why are you interested in our company?*

Similar interview questions:
- *What is it about our company that you find interesting or attractive?*
- *Is there a specific part of our company where you have interest in working?*
- *Are you interested in our company specifically or just in the job?*
- *Why do you want to work for us?*
- *What do you know about our company?*

Why the interviewer is asking this question:
The interviewer is asking this question to understand your motivation for applying to the company and to gauge your level of interest and research into the company. It also gives them insight into how well you align with the company's values, mission, and culture.

The best approach to answering this question:
Demonstrate your knowledge and understanding of the company, explain how your skills and experience align with the company's goals, and show enthusiasm for the company and the potential to grow within the organization.

An example of how to best answer this question
"I am highly interested in Google, both at a general level and specifically for the work being done in the department relevant to this role. With my extensive electrical engineering background, which is primarily software-oriented, and my recent experience working with Tesla, I believe my skills and expertise directly align with Google's requirements for this position

within the Self-Driving Car Project..."

Example:
"I have been following your company for some time now and I'm impressed with your innovation and commitment to sustainable technology. Your recent developments in renewable energy and electric vehicles align with my personal values, and I'm excited about the potential to work for a company that is making a positive impact on the environment. In addition, I've had the opportunity to speak with current employees and learn about the company culture, which I believe would be a great fit for my collaborative work style and desire for growth opportunities."

An example of how you should NOT answer this question:
"Honestly, I just need a job and your company seems like it has good benefits. Plus, I heard you're a big company, so that's cool."

The last thing you want to say is "for the money". This gives off the impression that your loyalty lies with the salary and not with the organization.

Your Role

Question: What do you think are the most important qualities for success in this role?

Similar interview questions:
- *What do you think is the most important skill for this role?*

Why the interviewer is asking this question:
The interviewer is asking this question to understand what qualities the candidate believes are necessary to excel in the role. This can give the interviewer insight into whether the candidate has done their research about the position and the company, and also whether their personal values and strengths align with the requirements of the job.

The best approach to answering this question:
Be specific and show how your experience and skills align with the job requirements. Start by researching the job description and the company culture, then highlight the qualities that are important for success in the role. Back up your answer with examples from your previous experiences or achievements, highlighting how those qualities contributed to your success.

Strong communication skills, attention to detail, and the ability to work collaboratively in a team environment are the most important qualities for success in this role. You could explain that you have experience in all of these areas and provide specific projects or accomplishments that demonstrate these characteristics.

An example of how to best answer this question:

"I believe that in this role, qualities such as strong communication skills, attention to detail, and ability to work collaboratively are important for success. As a result, I have worked on developing these skills through my previous roles and experiences. For example, in my last job, I was responsible for managing a team of five people and regularly communicated project goals and objectives, which required strong communication skills. My attention to detail helped me catch errors before they became problems, and my collaborative nature helped me work effectively with team members to ensure project deadlines were met."

Example:

"I believe that effective communication, attention to detail, and teamwork are crucial for success in this role. Throughout my career, I have honed my skills in these areas and have successfully completed projects that required these qualities. For instance, in my previous job, I collaborated with a team to deliver a project that required close attention to detail and clear communication to ensure that all deliverables were met on time. We worked together to identify and solve any issues that arose, and as a result, we delivered a high-quality product that met or exceeded our client's expectations. Overall, I am confident that my experience and abilities make me well-suited for this role."

An example of how you should not answer this question:
"I think the most important quality for success in this role is being able to work hard and get things done. I'm a hard worker and I always get the job done, so I think I would be great for this position."

Career Choice

Question: ***Why did you choose this career?***

Similar interview questions:
- *Why did you decide to become a _____?*
- *What factors influenced you to choose this career path?*
- *Why do you want to become a _____?*
- *Why do you want this job?*
- *Why are you applying for this job?*
- *Why are you here?*

Why the interviewer is asking this question:
The interviewer wants to understand your motivation for choosing your career path and to determine if your values and interests align with the requirements of the job you are applying for.

The best approach to answering this question:
Be honest and specific about what drew you to this career and how it aligns with your values and interests. Highlight any relevant skills or experiences that make you a strong candidate for the position.

Think about the factors which influenced your decision in advance. Include the positive influences, not the negative ones. If there were specific people who influenced your career choice, it adds a personal touch to your story.

An example of how to best answer this question
"In my first year of college, I chose Accounting as my major and dedicated my time and effort to excel in it. It wasn't until I landed an internship during my third

year that I found my passion for tax accounting. My mentor during the internship played a significant role in helping me gain a deeper understanding of the field and guiding me towards a clear career plan even after graduation."

Example of how you should NOT answer this question:
"I chose this career because it pays well, and it seems like an easy job that doesn't require too much effort. Plus, I heard the company has a great benefits package and lots of vacation time, so I thought it would be a good fit for me."

"The salary is high."

"I am jobless and desperate."

"I don't want to miss out on any opportunity."

Trends

Question: What do you do to stay up-to-date with industry trends?

Why the interviewer is asking this question:
The interviewer wants to know if you are committed to your field and if you are proactive in staying current with industry developments.

The best approach to answering this question:
Describe specific methods you use to stay informed about industry trends such as attending conferences, reading industry publications or blogs, participating in professional associations or online forums, and networking with colleagues.

An example of how to best answer this question:
"I like to stay current with what's going on in my industry, so I attend conferences and events and read blogs and publications. I'm also a member of professional organizations and online groups where I can network with others in my field. I find it beneficial to discuss current events with my colleagues and mentors, as well as seek their advice on new trends and techniques."

An example of how you should not answer this question:
"I don't really have a specific method for staying up-to-date with industry trends. I just kind of wait and see what happens or hear about things through my colleagues."

* * *

Question: *What important trends do you see in our industry?*

Why the interviewer is asking this question:
The interviewer wants to know if you understand the industry well, keep up with current trends, and can forecast future developments. They want to know if you've done your research, are truly interested in the field, and can help the company make strategic decisions and achieve growth.

The best approach to answering this question:
Stay informed: Keep up-to-date with industry news, articles, and reports to gain a solid understanding of current trends and future projections.

Be specific: Mention specific trends or changes in the industry that directly relate to the company and role you are interviewing for.

Show implications: Explain the potential impact of these trends on the company and suggest ways the organization can adapt or capitalize on them.

An example of how to best answer this question:
"In the [industry] field, I see a few key trends emerging. One significant trend is the growing importance of sustainability and environmentally friendly practices. Companies are being held accountable for their carbon footprint, and consumers are increasingly seeking eco-conscious products and services. Another trend is the rapid advancement of technology, such as AI and automation, which is transforming the way we work and streamlining processes. To stay competitive, I believe it is essential for [company name] to embrace

sustainable practices, invest in innovative technologies, and continuously adapt to the changing landscape."

An example of how you should not answer this question:
"I don't know, I haven't really been paying much attention to the industry news lately. I guess there are always some new trends happening, but I don't think it's that important for me to know about them. I'm sure the company has people who focus on that stuff, so I can just focus on doing my job."

Specific Experience

Question: What is your experience with sales?

Why the interviewer is asking this question:
The interviewer is asking this question to assess your experience in sales, which is a critical skill in many roles. They want to understand your ability to persuade customers, close deals, and generate revenue for the company.

The best approach to answering this question:
Provide specific examples of your experience in sales, highlighting your achievements and successes. Explain the sales techniques you used and how you managed to overcome any challenges that arose. Focus on how your sales experience can benefit the company and make you a valuable asset to the team.

An example of how to best answer this question:
"In my previous role as a sales representative, I was responsible for generating new business and maintaining relationships with existing clients. I consistently exceeded my sales targets by utilizing a consultative approach and building strong relationships with clients. For example, I developed a client-focused strategy that involved understanding their needs, providing tailored solutions, and following up with them regularly to ensure satisfaction. As a result, I increased sales revenue by 25% within the first six months of implementing the strategy."

An example of how you should not answer this question:
question:
"I have never worked in sales before, but I believe it's just about being persuasive and convincing customers to buy your product. It doesn't seem like it would be that difficult."

Qualification

Question: Your resume suggests that you may be over-qualified for this position. What is your opinion?

Why the interviewer is making this remark:
The interviewer might also be concerned that the candidate might get bored and leave the job soon.

When you are told that you are overqualified for a position, it is a warning sign that the employer may not fully comprehend the job requirements. They may assume that anyone can handle the role, or it could be an excuse not to hire you. Ideally, the interviewer should not make such a statement at all. If they do, it could indicate that they have not conducted the job analysis effectively. If the interviewer has done a thorough review of the CV, they would not have invited senior candidates for an interview when filling a junior role.

It happens in the IT industry where they think it is cheaper to get a fresh graduate. It ends up that they take longer to finish the project and the codes are buggy and badly documented. The quality of work is poor. If they care about quality of work, they would get good talent and pay them well. They save themselves a lot of headache down the road.

The best approach to answering this question:
Assure the interviewer that you are genuinely interested in the job and that you see it as an opportunity to contribute your skills and experience to the organization. Explain how this could be of benefit to them as you will be able to pick up things

around their office quicker and provide a faster return on their investment of hiring you.

Typically, individuals who are overqualified tend to leave a job when they can earn more money elsewhere. It's best to tailor your resume to the specific job you're applying for. If the job doesn't necessitate a master's degree and you possess one, it's recommended to exclude it from your resume. Downplay certain experiences and focus on making your resume meet the requirements of the job. During the interview, avoid mentioning your qualifications that are not relevant to the position.

An example of how to best answer this question:
"I understand that my experience may make me appear overqualified for the position, but please know that I am genuinely interested in this position. I am confident that my skills and expertise will have a significant impact in this organization. I'm looking forward to the opportunity to learn and grow in this role while working with such a great team. I am confident that my contribution will assist the company in meeting its objectives."

Here are some alternative responses to the statement:
- "I understand your concern, but I assure you that I am genuinely interested in this job and believe that my experience and skills can add value to the company."
- "I appreciate your feedback and understand that you may have reservations about my qualifications. However, I am confident that I can excel in this role and make a positive contribution to the team."

- "I understand that you may have concerns about my qualifications, but I believe that my skills and experience can bring a fresh perspective and new ideas to the team. Can we discuss how my qualifications can be an asset to the company?"
- "I appreciate your consideration and understand that you want the best fit for the job. However, I believe that my qualifications and experience can help me excel in this role and contribute to the company's success."

How do you respond to such a statement? How about posting a rhetorical question to the interviewer?

"If you require surgery, would you rather have a surgeon who is overqualified? Or do you trust a surgeon who isn't qualified but needs training? "When you go to the hospital, do you ask for the most underqualified doctor?"

If you know the company is doing badly, you can respond with, "Your company is losing money. Nobody is overqualified for this job."

If you don't want to sound sarcastic, you can ask them if there is a job that matches your qualification then. If they so much believe you are a qualified person, then they would very much like to have you in their company.

An example of how you should not answer this question:

"I know I'm overqualified, but I really need a job right now. I'm willing to take anything that pays the bills."

* * *

Question: *Your resume suggests that you may be under-qualified for this position. Do you think so?*

Why the interviewer is asking this question:
They are looking for candidates who can acknowledge their limitations, demonstrate a growth mindset, and convince the interviewer that they can quickly learn the necessary skills and contribute to the company's success.

The best approach to answering this question:
Reiterate your strengths and highlight your ability to learn quickly. Provide examples of how you've acquired new skills simply by observing others.

Be honest: Acknowledge the areas where you lack experience or qualifications, but emphasize your willingness to learn and try new things.

Highlight transferable skills: Showcase how your skills from previous experiences can be applied to this new role.

Show enthusiasm: Express your passion for the job and industry, indicating your motivation to excel and grow in the position.

Share examples: Provide specific instances where you have successfully overcome challenges, learned new skills, or adapted to new situations.

An example of how to best answer this question:
"I get that I may not have the exact experience you're looking for in [specific skill or qualification], but I think my background in [related experience or field] has

given me a good foundation in the industry. I'm a fast learner and I'm confident that I can pick up the skills I need to do well in this role. Actually, in my last job, I had to learn a new software system in a week and I was able to do it successfully by using online resources and asking my colleagues for help. I'm really passionate about [industry or job], and I'm excited to use my skills and grow with your company."

An example of how you should not answer this question:
"Well, I applied for this job because I thought it sounded interesting, but I didn't really look into the qualifications that much. I'm not sure why you called me in for an interview if you think I'm underqualified. I guess I can try to learn what I need to know, but it might take me a while, and I can't promise I'll be an expert right away."

You don't want to undervalue yourself by saying something like, "It's okay, we can negotiate the salary," or "You can offer me the lowest-paid job in the office." Avoid sounding desperate at all costs.